Theirs Be the Power

Between the workman and the master
there are frequent relations but no
real association. . . . I am of the
opinion, upon the whole, that the
manufacturing aristocracy which is
growing up under our eyes is one of
the harshest that ever existed in
the world. . . . if ever a permanent
inequality of conditions and aristocracy again penetrate into the world,
it may be predicted that this is
the gate by which they will enter.

—Alexis de Tocqueville

Harry M. Caudill

THEIRS BE THE POWER

The Moguls of
Eastern Kentucky

UNIVERSITY OF ILLINOIS PRESS

Urbana and Chicago

To the unborn, that numerous people
who will walk in our paths and claim
the places we now call our own

This book is printed on acid-free paper.

Library of Congress Cataloging in Publication Data

Caudill, Harry M., 1922—
  Theirs be the power.

  Includes bibliographical references and index.
  1. Wealth—Kentucky—History.   2. Capitalists and
financiers—Kentucky—History.   3. Kentucky—History.
4. Kentucky—Economic conditions.   5. Kentucky—
Social conditions.   6. Kentucky—Politics and government.   7. Coal mines and mining—Kentucky—History.
8. Energy industries—Kentucky—History.   I. Title.
HC107.K43W43   1983   332'.092'2   83-5771
ISBN 0-252-01029-9

Acknowledgments

THE WORK THAT PRODUCED this book extended over more than twenty years and owes much to many helpful people. A sincere debt of gratitude is due each of them.

To my wife, Anne Frye Caudill, I am obligated in a very special way. Her patient research in libraries, her endless hours at copying machines, and her toil at her typewriter entitle her to a claim of co-authorship. She rejected that right but I assert it nonetheless, for her contributions caused the book to emerge from the presses.

Thanks are due to Anne Campbell, librarian of the Appalachian Collection at the University of Kentucky's Margaret I. King Library, and to the kind people in the Interlibrary Loan Service. They helped me accumulate two drawers full of research materials dealing with the history of the central Appalachians. Their unflagging zeal and courtesy demonstrated a genuine interest.

Al Smith, a Kentucky newspaperman and for three years federal co-chairman of the Appalachian Regional Commission, is a staunch friend of the Appalachian people. He aided and encouraged my work most generously and in a way that all authors esteem and cherish.

The research that made this book possible was aided by a generous grant from the Appalachian Community Service Network. I am happy to express my appreciation for that interest and support.

Finally, a word is due those other friends of historians: the dealers in rare old books. Somehow they found for me scores of musty, obscure, long-forgotten but highly important volumes from other times. Without such works the story of the Appalachian coal fields would have to go untold. It is a comfort to have many of these books on my own shelves, safe for a time from incinerators and landfills.

Harry M. Caudill
Whitesburg, Kentucky
1983

Contents

Eastern Kentucky, showing selected features mentioned in the text.

Introduction

EASTERN KENTUCKY HAS BEEN much in the news for a long time and for many reasons. Its 13,302 square miles of rugged mountains, low razor-back hills, and narrow valleys are part of the Appalachians, and Americans have demonstrated a prolonged fascination with the land and the people of the southern and central portions of that ancient range.

Reams of paper and torrents of ink have been expended on the "quaint" people of the Kentucky highlands. They first caught the attention of the nation during the Civil War, when their isolated society was shattered by marching armies and ferocious partisanship. There were few neutrals in the hills after Fort Sumter; in many counties civil government dissolved,[1] and the big war led to innumerable little ones which were chronicled as "feuds." Then, in the 1890's, local-color writers began making their way along the atrocious trails that passed for roads and described their finds in scores of articles. One of the first of these gentry, Will Wallace Harney, gave the region a label that has endured in the popular mind: "a strange land and a peculiar people."[2] The string of appellations grew in the half-century that followed. The hill people were described as picturesque, quaint, primitive, suspicious, narrow-minded, ignorant, and of low mentality. But not all writers were detractors. Some found the mountaineers to be brave, chivalrous, noble, generous, free-spirited, splendid Anglo-Saxons, and guardians and preservers of our British heritage.[3]

Most often the highland people have attracted the nation's attention because of tragedy and misfortune, as when the region is lashed by a deadly flood, or a coal mine explosion devastates

a community, or a labor struggle convulses a coal field. Sometimes the newspeople are attracted by malign conditions that
appear especially stark when seen amid the somber hills. In the
heyday of the mid-1960's "Great Society," reporters trekked
into the eastern Kentucky outback to photograph poverty and
squalor.[4] When poverty lost its vogue and environmentalism
became the grand new cause, they returned to capture the spec-
tacle of strip-mined mountains and sulfurous, silt-choked,
trash-strewn streams. In 1973, when the Arabs embargoed oil
shipments to the United States and coal prices on the spot market rose by as much as 700 percent in a single year, the media
pilgrims came to tell the tale of paupers turned into princes. Instant millionaires explained to all and sundry how they had acquired fortunes and retired, or moved out of the hills to become
bankers and horse breeders.[5] In due time the coal boom dissolved and the cameramen reappeared, this time to relate the
tale of woe caused by a coal glut in the midst of an oft-
proclaimed "energy crisis."

   The published story of eastern Kentucky has been one of
almost unrelieved gloom. Despite periodic fuel shortages and
the resulting booms, the people remain poor. Though the 1970's
saw Kentucky surpass West Virginia to become the nation's
largest coal producer, mountain people shared only minimally
in the prosperity. In 1976 the state ranked forty-fourth in per
capita income, and the five poorest counties in America were in
the Kentucky hills. In one of them (Owsley) 2,565 of the 5,200
inhabitants received food stamps, and 62 percent of its population lived below the federally determined poverty level.[6] In the
most prosperous county, Pike, which during the coal boom of
1973-75 had been hailed as "a little Saudia Arabia of coal," 23
percent of the residents were receiving various forms of welfare.
Numerous costly federal rescue programs and a period of high
coal prices had strewn the narrow valleys with new mobile
homes, clogged the county seats with large and expensive cars,
financed several hundred impressive residences, but changed
little else. The schools were still dreary and underfinanced.
Taxes on the extractive coal, oil, gas, and quarrying industries
remained at trifling levels. Entire counties with large coal industries lacked any kind of hospital facilities. Public health was dis-

mal. It was estimated that half of the people had intestinal worms, and the region was plagued with extremely high rates of heart disease, epilepsy, diabetes, and depression.[7] Psychiatrists coined a new term—the "eastern Kentucky syndrome"—for a chronically depressed and passive state of mind which they averred to be totally disabling.

Amid this welter of economic and social chaos, of poverty, passivity, and dependence, there was another and little-known world of prosperity, ease, and power. This was the world of the coal barons—the people who owned the fabulous mineral riches of Appalachian Kentucky. For more than fifteen years segments of the press have struggled to reveal this world of Appalachian opulence amid Appalachian destitution. In April, 1965, *Dun's Review*, an investment magazine, described the startling prosperity of the eastern Kentucky mineral industries, pointing out that the nation's most profitable investor-owned corporations were obscure eastern Kentucky land companies. Four months later the *Louisville Courier-Journal* described Kentucky's primitive system of tax assessment and collection. The tax commissioners were shown to have only the scantiest knowledge of local mineral wealth. They were not aware of how many acres the land corporations owned, or of the quality or quantity of the underlying coal, oil, and gas deposits. The writer, Kyle Vance, showed with great clarity that while the mineral industries were generating a "flood of profit," the state was receiving the merest "trickle of taxes." A year later James C. Millstone explored this paradox of poverty amid riches in two powerful articles in the *St. Louis Post-Dispatch*. He detailed the curious fact that in impoverished eastern Kentucky, where federal dollars were being enlisted in a "war on poverty," gigantic and immensely profitable corporations were escaping almost untaxed, thereby assuring more poverty.[8]

In short, the rich were in total and unchallenged control of the Appalachian coal fields. The region and its people had been and were being exploited in a manner that might have reddened the cheeks of Attila the Hun. The valleys were strewn with rotting coal "camps" which their builders had abandoned after mechanization of the mines in the 1950's eliminated the need for hand labor. The low taxes on mineral resources held schools, courts, law enforcement, and public health services to minimal levels. Trash disposal consisted of throwing unwanted refuse in the streams. Public officials at all levels fawned over the mineral industrialists while pitching welfare crumbs to the swarming paupers. Such a medieval situation, unthinkable elsewhere among "advanced" nations, raises the serious possibility that it was all brought about deliberately by the region's landlords in their single-minded pursuit of profits.[9]

At least one Kentucky politician had the courage to attack the problem head on. In 1923 Alben Barkley sought the Democratic gubernatorial nomination, promising to levy a "percentage" tax on minerals "severed" from the state's soil and to use the revenue to finance an effective and uniform school system. He castigated the coal moguls before scores of audiences: "You can't get a school bill through the legislature without going to the coal lobby for their consent. If you want a road past the school house you must see them. I propose to take the filthy hands of the coal combine from the throat of Kentucky!" Barkley, an accomplished politician and a powerful orator, later became the U.S. Senate majority leader and Harry Truman's vice-president—but he never became governor of Kentucky. The "coal combine" rallied its forces against him. The great land-owning corporations and their lease-holding operators, the steel corporations, the oil and gas companies, the railroad and pipe-line companies, the barge companies, and the electric utilities formed a militant and invincible phalanx. As two insightful politicians, Jesse Unruh and Lyndon Johnson, would later remind us, "Money is the mother's milk of politics." In 1923 the economic muscle was braced solidly against Barkley. His defeat taught him a lesson which he expressed in a private conversation thirty years later: "You can't win elections on issues!"

In the six decades since Barkley's defeat, billions of tons of Kentucky coal and most of the oil in the state's shallow deposits have been extracted. The state continues to be an important producer of natural gas. Billions of tons of coal remain in the hills, and prominent oil geologists have written that vast deposits of petroleum lie deep under the Appalachian overfold, valley, and adjacent plateaus.[10] Oil companies have quietly moved in, buying huge acreages and leasing much more. The coal industry is changing as coal companies become subsidiaries of petroleum companies. The "filthy hands" of the combine have become larger, and stronger, and their grip on the state's throat grows more oppressive.[11]

The primary purpose of this book is not to analyze Kentucky's economic and political problems or to propose solutions for them. The library shelves are already replete with such studies. My aim is to explore a fascinating period in the state's history from a perspective that historians have consistently ignored. I seek to remove the shadows of obscurity from the names and works of a generation of industrial moguls who transformed a remote and impoverished hinterland into the nation's most productive coal field. They turned a backwoods people—the Kentucky "hillbillies"—into industrial workers, removing thousands of them from their tiny farms in mountain coves and resettling them in a few solid, well-planned towns and in many scabrous camps that were hideous slums from the beginning. I shall discuss the legacy of economic and political power that has come down to us from those times and how it affects the present generations of Kentuckians.

The word *mogul* has been chosen deliberately because the dictionary assigns it a meaning that precisely fits those dead and vanished industrialists: a "rich and powerful man." The men who industrialized the hundreds of valleys in Appalachian Kentucky were, indeed, both rich and powerful. They were "men of enterprise," goodly of girth, and the gold chains that gleamed across their vests secured costly, many-jeweled watches. They lived in regal mansions and (in those days before the corporate jet) traveled in immaculately kept private railroad cars. They ate the best foods and stocked their cellars with superb champagnes and costly vintage wines. Their walls were bedecked with diplomas from good colleges, and their sons and daughters studied at prestigious campuses. Their frequent trips to Europe were taken amid the luxuries of ocean liners. When business called them from their baronial halls, they relaxed in hotel suites. They knew presidents, congressmen, and governors and could open doors to the innermost sanctums of power. Many of them combined business with political office and were called "governor," "senator," or "congressman" in their own right. They were attended by the best physicians and counseled by the wisest lawyers. They collected corporate directorships by the dozens. Most of them were bankers, who manipulated the aggregate funds of entire communities, sometimes, of broad regions. Some of them were almost scandalously intermarried to kinswomen. Their progeny invariably found spouses among the offspring of other moguls.

Some of these moguls inherited great wealth and then merely strove to increase it; others were born poor and accumulated fortunes with sure and relentless hands. In the days before the United States levied income or inheritance taxes, when myriad workmen provided hard labor for low wages, it was surprisingly easy to become rich. Those fortunes were in dollars backed by gold, and each of them packed a fantastic wallop. At the turn of the century a dollar sent a miner deep underground to shovel coal for ten consecutive hours—and at the end of the day he was likely to feel gratitude to the "big bosses" for their generosity.

The moguls were men of means and power and ostentation, but not all remained so. Some met disaster in the stock market crash of 1929 and ended their days working at jobs their more fortunate fellows charitably made for them. Others were ruined by a coal market they had glutted beyond all reason. In short, they lived grandly but dangerously.

When they turned their attention and capital to eastern Kentucky, it became putty in their hands. At their insistence railroads penetrated the meandering valleys of the Cumberland, Big Sandy, and Kentucky Rivers and scores of tributaries. Power plants rose to light homes and energize mines. Thousands of look-alike houses popped up in rows along narrow bottomlands and around steep hills. Tipples were built by the dozen, by the hundred. From near and far, from farms and cities, thousands of men came to dig coal. Immigrant ships brought strangers from a score of lands. The culture of a broad region was drastically battered and reshaped. European peasants and Appalachian scratch farmers worked side by side, totally dependent on the company commissary for credit and groceries. Self-reliant mountain people whose ancestors had lived free for generations before the battle of King's Mountain became, within a decade, company dependent. In old age most of them would become government dependent.

The moguls altered people as easily as they reshaped the land on which those people lived. They loved to call themselves philanthropists; many of them did, in fact, bestow substantial sums on museums, libraries, churches, and colleges—all located outside the Kentucky coal fields. But in truth they were a hard lot, viewing their workmen with contempt at worst and with good-natured condescension at best. They demanded not only the miner's labor but also his ballot and a serflike obedience. When the miners revolted, as they often did, the "philanthropists" marshaled the power of state and federal bayonets to "restore order," and company-paid guards and sheriff's deputies shot the recalcitrant and the "ungrateful."

In launching their immense projects the moguls retained a high opinion of themselves as regional benefactors who made it possible for poor people to have shelter and food. Because the poor, they believed, were of an inferior order and easy to satisfy, the paternalistic moguls marveled that their workmen were not always satisfied with the world that had been created for them. As church members they deemed themselves social pillars and doers of good. As capitalists they commanded money and men in the forging of a greater America. They worked patriotically to remake America to their liking and, as they believed, for its everlasting betterment. One of them, George F. Baer, wrote a letter in which he indiscreetly stated a philosophical principle in which they all steadfastly believed: "The rights and interests of the laboring man will be protected and cared for . . . by the Christian men to whom God . . . has given the control of the property interest of the country."[12] Super mogul John Davison Rockefeller, Sr., expressed it more succinctly: "GOD gave me my money."[13] Simply put, the moguls believed in the Divine Right of Cash, and their subsidized clergymen preached that doctrine from countless pulpits.

The work of the moguls can best be judged on a visit to the Kentucky hills.

It should not be inferred that the moguls were the first to mine coal in eastern Kentucky. Small-scale mining was underway in Lee and Estill Counties before 1800, when fuel was floated down the Kentucky River in barges to buyers in the central and northern parts of the state. Milton Freeze, Richard Deering, and William Mellen opened mines and built camps in the Big Sandy Valley at Louisa, Peach Orchard, Betsey Layne, and Paintsville a decade before the Civil War.[14] These pioneering efforts, impressive for their time, failed because of inadequate transportation facilities and wartime disruptions. Strip mining was practiced in Laurel County as early as 1870.[15] After the tracks of the Chatteroi Railway Company reached Richardson, a mining camp at Peach Orchard, production increased; in 1888 the tiny line hauled away 137,500 tons. These early entrepreneurs were trailblazers for the moguls, and without their accomplishments the moguls might not have come. They were ambitious and hard-driving men, but neither their financial resources, aspirations, nor accomplishments mark them as rich and powerful.

Any reader who has not already done so should explore America's great age of fortune-building before proceeding further into these pages. That age extended from about 1860 to the stock market crash of 1929. The industrialization of eastern Kentucky was an almost insignificant part of a titanic, many-faceted drama of money, mansions, railroads, oil wells, mines, and factories that played across oceans and continents. Of the many fine books on the subject, three are especially important, providing essential background for understanding the men and circumstances that made eastern Kentucky as it is today: *The Robber Barons* and *The Politicos* by Matthew Josephson, and *The Age of the Moguls* by Stewart Holbrook.[16] In these works one can meet the great industrial capitalists who reigned over America for seven decades and whose tenets of faith were a monetary gold standard, high tariffs, and opposition to labor unions. On these rocks they built their world.

ONE

Why the Moguls Came

FOR THIRTY YEARS after the mid-1880's the Cumberland Plateau and the Cumberland mountain ranges swarmed with land speculators. Some were jobbers buying land for resale at substantially higher prices to companies that would "develop" it by extracting the minerals. Typical of these was Griffith Kelly of Urbana, Ohio, who acquired 67,000 acres in Breathitt County and advertised the great value of his property in 1885.[1] Others were agents of families or investor cartels who planned to hold the lands for leasing to mining companies. Their income would reach them as "royalties" paid by operators—perhaps ten cents per ton of coal mined and 12½ percent of the well-head price of oil and gas. Still others sought lands for companies that would mine it themselves. This latter group included International Harvester, United States Steel, Ford Motor Company, and a number of electric utilities.

It is important that we understand the value of this rugged country as it was perceived by bankers and industrialists of that era. For nearly a century writers and lecturers had been describing the steep hills, retreating forest, weather-beaten frontier-style cabins, and the poverty of most of the inhabitants.[2] In this grim backwoods the moguls saw prospects for great riches.

The region was without a decent road, and the chief means of travel were afoot, on a horse or mule, or in a crude mule-drawn sled. Railroads had ventured into the foothills after timber and had reached Whitley County west of Cumberland Gap to open a portion of the Cumberland coal field. But the entire heartland consisting of a dozen counties was almost as hard to penetrate as it had been in the winter of 1767-68, when Daniel Boone, lost and weary, spent several weeks huddled under a cliff in what later became Floyd County.

The highland people attached little value to the minerals reputed to lie beneath their lands, and the vast majority were eager to sell on the buyers' terms. The rich and powerful moguls knew infinitely more about the region than the people who inhabited it. The information that set off the land buying was available to anyone with enough ambition to read the geological and mineralogical studies that had been accumulating since a "reconnaisance" was authorized by the legislature in 1838. William W. Mather of New York, a descendant of the renowned preacher Cotton Mather, was the state's first official geologist. A former professor of chemistry, mineralogy, and geology at the United States Military Academy, he brought outstanding competence to his work in the hills. In his report to the governor and legislature he estimated the eastern coal field to cover 7,000 square miles. He described the general quality of the various deposits and noted the location of limestone and iron-bearing rock.

In subsequent years Mather's findings were enlarged and refined by his able successor, Dr. David Dale Owen. In 1873 Dr. Nathaniel Southgate Shaler of Harvard was employed to bring Kentucky's survey up to date. A scientist who in 1895 was elected president of the Geological Society of America, Shaler spent seven years locating, mapping, and analyzing the state's mineral riches. After 1880 any literate person could know what those mineral resources were and where they lay. Much work remained in confirming the state's studies by core drilling and driving mine shafts, but the basic surveying task was complete. J. R. Proctor expanded Shaler's work from 1880 to 1892. The 3,020 pages of his report indicated probable oil and gas deposits and greatly extended the known limits of the eastern Kentucky field.

Cumulatively these detailed documents included more than 8,000 pages and aroused the interest of industrialists in several states and in Great Britain. The field was shown to embrace 10,600 square miles and seven identifiable coal beds or seams known in various localities by no fewer than 190 names. The coal lay in thirty-three recognizable measures. The deposits then contained about 35 billion tons, of which more than half lay in Upper Elk Horn Nos. 1, 2, and 3, Fire Clay, Fire Clay Rider, Amburgey, and Hazard No. 7. The coal ranged in thickness from fourteen inches to eleven feet.[3]

The Elk Horn vein was so called because Richard M. Broas found samples of coal in Elkhorn Creek when he camped there as a captain in the Union Army. Analysis showed this coal to be superb, excellent for coking, rich in by-product gas, and low in sulfur. (An outcropping of it was identified by Albert R. Crandall of the Kentucky Geological Survey on Elkhorn Creek of the Big Sandy River in 1881.) Broas believed it to be the best coal in the United States. In 1881 he returned to the Big Sandy as an agent of two prominent glass-making industrialists, Edward D. Libby and his brother-in-law, William S. Walbridge, both of Toledo, Ohio. Broas hoped to find his peerless coal at Louisa or just above the forks of the Big Sandy. Disappointed in the quality of the mineral in that area, Libby and Walbridge lost interest in the project, and in the autumn Broas extended his search to Millers Creek in Johnson County. This time he was sponsored by a New England group that included Nathaniel Stone Simpkins, John Murray Forbes, and Warren Delano, grandfather of Franklin Delano Roosevelt. Broas bought 10,000 acres for them on Rockcastle Fork of Millers Creek. Later he came to the Ash Camp section of Pike County. In the fall of 1883, at Joe's Branch, he found the princess of coals which he had known from his old creek-bed scavenging had to exist. This he called the "true Elk Horn," a superb deposit sprawling north and eastward, over tens of thousands of acres, each of them capable of yielding 12,000 tons. In that year he floated a stupendous solid block of his glittering "stone coal" to Louisville by barge and displayed it at the Southern Exposition. The exhibit was more than eight feet long and as thick as the marvelous vein from which it had been wrested. The tasks of extracting and transporting it were major engineering accomplishments carried out in a rugged, almost roadless wilderness. In 1886-87 Broas bought 11,000 acres on the headwaters of Elkhorn Creek and adjoining streams, thereby acquiring the best part of Kentucky's finest coal seam.[4]

Broas's activities gave credence to the optimistic assessments made by the state's geologists, and coal and steel circles began to buzz with assertions that the Kentucky hills contained as much coal as England. The greater part of these immense deposits were in the counties of Johnson, Floyd, Pike, Letcher, Harlan, Bell, Knox, Perry, Knott, Leslie, Clay, Martin, and Breathitt. On the basis of experience in older mining fields in Pennsylvania and West Virginia, it was believed that only the Black Mountain would be burdened with deadly methane gas. Since most of the seams sloped slightly, it was anticipated that the operations would be largely self-draining. Then, too, the surveys indicated the presence of iron and (on the northwest slope of Pine Mountain) huge deposits of limestone. In short, here were concentrated all the resources necessary for a successful steel industry.

In 1892 a wildcat driller named Louis Gormley brought in a highly productive gas well on Beaver Creek in Floyd County. Geologists promptly surmised that petroleum was present also—petroleum and the chemical-rich brines which were becoming so important to a broad spectrum of evolving industries.

Not only did the mountaineer lack fundamental knowledge about his land but, more often than not, he simply did not own it. While Kentucky had suffered from abominable land titles ever since it was a part of Virginia, in the mountains the difficulties were infinitely compounded. The insecurity of mountain land titles discouraged improvements and tended to bind the mountaineer to a primitive and unproductive agriculture. For a century the threat of dispossession had hung over thousands of mountain families. Under such circumstances they were tempted to neglect fences and houses, to do just enough to get by, and simply to wait and see what would happen. This situation grew out of the Revolutionary War and Virginia's efforts to reward the officers who had served her so faithfully during that long struggle. The Old Dominion lacked money to pay the claims of her defenders but held title to an immense territory. Because the land was wild, unimproved, and nearly worthless, the state issued warrants for giant tracts. For example, General John Preston received 100,000 acres "on the waters of Sandy," and scores of others were given grants for smaller but still vast districts. Preston hired a family of fearless mercenary Indian fighters—Mathias, Adam, Valentine, and Acquilla Harman—to build a fort on the Big Sandy in the late 1780's and to secure the region against raids by the Shawnees in Ohio. He sent John Graham, surveyor and "land locator," to "spy out" the valley and choose suitable holdings. Graham, carrying out his mission under the protection of the Harman rifles, laid out Preston's Station, a backwoods bastion which became the town of Prestonsburg.[5]

Graham spent a decade in the employ of Virginia war veterans, locating and surveying a total of approximately a half-million acres in eastern Kentucky. Other surveyors joined in the task, including Daniel Boone, who marked out a 50,000-acre spread in the territory that became Owsley County.[6] By 1792 nearly all of the hill country had been investigated, surveyed, and patented in the names of Virginians who would seldom or never visit their large but practically valueless holdings.

When Kentucky became a state in 1792, Virginia remembered her veterans and required the new "commonwealth" to expressly covenant in its constitution that it would uphold the validity of those military grants. When two subsequent constitutions were adopted, the same provision was included. The future of these grants depended on the ability of their proprietors to attract settlers who would buy farms. Unfortunately, few settlers had money, and by 1800 more hospitable lands were available in Ohio and Indiana. When Graham held a lot sale at Preston's Station, one lot, a prime building site, brought a mere seventy-five cents.

The first permanent settlers began filtering through the mountain gaps from Virginia and North Carolina and drifting up from central Kentucky around 1790. Most of these newcomers found river or creek bottoms, surveyed a few hundred or a thousand acres, and applied for title papers. The real difficulties began after 1800, when a huge flow of poor hill people from the North Carolina, South Carolina, Virginia, and Tennessee back country began pouring into the region. Exceedingly lackadaisical about such things as land titles, taxes, and laws, they built houses wherever fertile lands enticed them; predictably, thousands simply "squatted" within the Virginia grants. They ignored the surveyors' hack marks on the boundary trees, scorning the claims of distant owners when their own needs were immediate. But those surveyors' marks were not forgotten, and as the generations passed and the people multiplied and spread up the creeks and into the hollows, the nagging certainty persisted that someday, in God's good time, "the law" would summon them to their doors with writs of eviction. Then the ancient military grants would prevail over their squatter's rights, and they would be compelled to abandon the lands and houses of a century. Even the buried bones of their ancestors would pass to strangers.

Imagine, then, the delight of most mountaineers when the anticipated strangers came to their gates not to bid them to be gone, but to buy with gold the minerals said to repose beneath the lands described in their doubtful deeds. An annual burden lay in raising the five or ten dollars most families paid to the county tax collector. Now gullible "furriners" offered new gold pieces fresh from government mints for substances most people had never seen and had no intention of using. (Indeed, they often doubted that those substances existed.) Besides, the deeds they were asked to sign would have had to be defended against those lurking Virginia claimants—and the Virginians would probably win! In most instances a few hundred dollars, a sum most highland people had never dreamed of possessing, could be obtained for the sale of mineral rights.

Thus there would meet in a fantastically valuable mineral field those two characters so dear to the hearts of real estate lawyers, "the willing buyer and the willing seller, in a free and voluntary trade."

Finally, it must be noted that for the financial and industrial empire-builders the era was one of boundless accomplishment and self-confidence. Railroads had spanned the continent, and America's grain, hides, and lumber were flowing to the ends of the earth. Rockefeller's Standard Oil trust was flourishing, piling up a score of huge fortunes. Steel and iron were booming and the United States was moving to world leadership in both steel and coal. Petroleum was still used mainly for lubrication and lighting. Most illuminating and heating gas was manufactured from coal, which also powered electric plants, navies, passenger ships, trains, home furnaces, and fireplaces. The population was about 90 million and growing steadily, with new immigrants arriving daily. The need for coal, coke, gas, chemicals, and steel appeared certain to grow exponentially during the new century. No one anticipated sixty years of oil so cheap and abundant that it would drive competing fuels from a half-dozen major markets. Atomic energy was not yet even a faint gleam in some physicist's eye. The moguls could reasonably suppose that the market for their black carbon lumps would always grow, that prices would creep ever upward, and that hillbillies and Europe's expatriates would continue to toil with gratitude and diligence to keep the coal trains rolling.

It was a propitious time for mogul and mountaineer alike. The future promised dividends to one and to the other wages. In an imperfect world, few can ask for more.

TWO

Middlesborough:
The Magic City

IN THE FALL OF 1968, on a visit to Ireland, my wife
and I stopped at a pub to sample the black porter and hear some
authentic Irish songs. The fiddler, the piper, and the guitarist
were in fine fettle and were greeted with whistles and foot-
stomping. After the inevitable tuning up and exchange of banter
with the crowd, they began a song known to practically every
mountaineer:

> O, the Cumberland Gap, it ain't very fur
> From the little old town of Middlesbur;
>
> The town was built by an English chap
> Straight down under the Cumberland Gap.

The ditty could not have been received with greater enthusiasm
anywhere in Bell County, Kentucky. The musicians strung it out
to a dozen verses, some of which we had never before heard.

Nor is it strange that a little city "straight down under the
Cumberland Gap" should have become known in far countries.
Middlesborough was indeed built by an English chap (or, more
accurately, a Scot), and the manner in which it came into existence in so unlikely a place captured the imagination of the
English-speaking world. Built at breakneck speed and with
boundless optimism, it almost died in equally spectacular
fashion. Whatever else we may learn from the incredible story
of this town, we certainly discover that great booms end in great
busts, and that the prudent man bridles his greed, takes his
profits, and gets out before the bubble bursts.

Cumberland Gap is an ancient pass in Cumberland Mountain. When Kentucky was being settled the trail that ran
through it, and northwest to the Bluegrass and the Ohio River,
was known as Boone's Trace. Daniel Boone and a score of
sturdy axemen cut the road in 1775, from Long Island on the
Holston River to Boonesborough on the Kentucky. The "trace"
was just that when Boone completed it—a narrow path a few
feet wide from which the brush had been cleared and the most
troublesome tree branches hacked away. Rough but clearly visible, it beckoned multitudes of backwoods people westward to
the promised land.

Boone and his associates were employed by Colonel Richard
Henderson and a newly created corporation called the Transylvania Company. It had "bought" 20 million acres from the
Cherokees and planned to settle the land as an old-fashioned
proprietorship—an outmoded scheme that neither the backwoodsmen nor the Commonwealth of Virginia would tolerate.
The company collapsed in Kentucky's first great economic debacle. For decades thereafter the Wilderness Road was alive with
men, women, and children pushing through the Gap. Most were
afoot, though some rode horses or clung to the backs of cattle.
They drove before them lean cows, small droves of razor-back
hogs, and a few oxen. Their possessions were axes, skillets,
spinning wheels, and rifles. Most were the upland people of
North Carolina and of Virginia's great valley. They settled the
Kentucky Bluegrass, then pushed on into Indiana and Ohio.
They were obstreperous, quarrelsome, quick-tempered, and
stubborn. A few were preachers; nearly all were believers—in
Heaven and Hell, in Jesus Christ, in Salvation. They were hospitable with their meager possessions, tended to scorn schools,
and disliked taxes and government. About 1800 a new tide
poured in from the Virginia Blue Ridge and Tidewater regions,
mingling with the older flows, then turning aside to settle the
Kentucky hills and mountains.

The descendants of these settlers remained in the hills, little
altered by the intervening generations, when the Civil War
brought armies and immense strings of supply wagons to the
Cumberland Gap. Soldiers reported seeing mountain men
dressed in coonskin caps and carrying flintlock rifles. Some-

times these frontiersmen avenged themselves on the soldiers
who plundered them for "forage," ambushing the trailbound
columns with deadly rifle fire. In an interval when a Confederate army occupied the Gap, Indians were brought in from the
southern plains to stalk and kill the pro-Union "bushwhackers."
Some Indians returned with bloody scalps as trophies, but
others did not return at all. In his native hills the highlander was
a formidable foe.[1]

After the war the mountaineers resumed their old routines in-
sofar as they could. They sent droves of range-fed hogs and cattle through the Gap to markets in "the old settlements." (The
rooting swine reduced the worn trail to a nearly impassable
"hog road.") Migrations carried many people westward to the
Ozarks. The Cumberland Gap and the historic trace lapsed into
silence. In their solitude the people farmed a little, drank home-
distilled whiskey, repeated the old traditions to their children,
and whittled. The valley of Yellow Creek, which ran down from
the north face of Cumberland Mountain and found its way to
the Cumberland River, slept quietly. Time and America seemed
to have abandoned them all—stream, valley, mountain, and
people—to "the rime of centuries."[2]

The boundary lines of three states—Virginia, Tennessee, and
Kentucky—meet at Cumberland Gap. In 1886 a tiny hamlet of
six crude log cabins and humble frame houses bore the name of
the historic pass. The nearest railroad was thirteen miles away.
Schools, banks, stage performances, electricity, and telegraphs
were, for all practical purposes, as remote as Mars.

In that year a most unlikely personage appeared at Cumberland Gap. He rode a fine, sturdy horse—and, in truth, the horse
needed all its strength, for his rider was accustomed to fine food
and was, in consequence, a man of ample girth.

Alexander Alan Arthur was one of the most memorable figures ever to cross Kentucky's threshold. In his background and
outlook he was everything the highland people were not. Arthur
was forty-one in 1886. Born in Glasgow, he had been taken to
Montreal as a child, and he grew up in Canada. His parents
died when he was twenty, and he went to work to support and
educate his younger brothers and sisters. On his father's side he
was related to former President Chester A. Arthur; his mother

was a distant kinswoman of the author and statesman Thomas
Babington Macaulay, whose "Horatius at the Bridge" had en-
thralled legions of schoolboys.

As a young man Arthur went back to Scotland and married
Mary Forrest, a queenly beauty from Birkenhead. Fitting well
into Scottish society, the youthful charmer joined the famous
104th Highland Regiment. He taught some of his friends
lacrosse, and they played it so enthusiastically that he organized
the Caledonia Lacrosse Club.

Tiring of Scotland, he went to Sweden and Norway for a year
or two. He then immigrated again, this time to Boston as representative of an English steelmaker. When Mary died, he found a
new wife, Nellie Goodwin, a proper Bostonian with important
family connections. Ever on the outlook for opportunities to
build a fortune, Arthur gravitated to the North Carolina and
Tennessee mountains to supervise a Scottish-owned lumber
company. In North Carolina he met a number of the eastern
moguls who vacationed at the fast-growing resort city of Asheville. There he read an article by an inveterate romanticist,
James Lane Allen, extolling the natural resources of the Cumberlands.[3] As an agent of the Richmond & Danville Railroad
Company, he came to the Gap to consider the feasibility of extending the company's line from Morristown, Tennessee, into
the Kentucky Cumberlands. The project was awesome because
of the almost unbelievably rough terrain. A tunnel through
Cumberland Mountain was inescapable, and the directors
quailed at the millions it would cost.

Arthur had the good fortune to find lodgings a few miles
south of the Gap, in the home of Dr. James M. Harbison. When
Arthur told Harbison why he had come, the doctor leaped to
his aid, pointing out the mighty wall of Cumberland Mountain,
the boldly upthrust crag called the Pinnacle, the less threatening
height of Poor Valley Ridge, and describing the sullen slopes of
Pine Mountain a dozen miles to the northeast. The doctor
thought that the railroad could be built, and that Alexander
Alan Arthur was the man to build it.

The next morning Arthur followed the grim old road up the
south slope of the Cumberland, past Poor Valley Ridge and
through the historic Gap. On the way he stopped to talk to a

miller whose ancient water-powered stones ground corn and wheat. He dismounted to inspect a silent and deserted iron forge that had supplied an earlier generation of mountaineers with metal for guns, kettles, axes, and wagon wheel rims. Coming fresh from a busy modern world, Arthur found this new setting eerie but charming.

Along Yellow Creek he talked to people about land prices and the extent of good virgin forests that remained in outlying areas. At his request some of the young men showed him a coal "bank" where the more enterprising families dug fuel for their fireplaces. They rode with him to the beetling cliffs and broke off pieces of rock rich in iron ore—trophies that joined the lumps of coal in Arthur's saddlebags.[4]

A portion of the valley of Yellow Creek is round like a bullet hole. (Geologists say this basin was made when something from space struck the ridge that runs between the Pine and Cumberland Mountains.) The circular valley captivated Arthur. "Here," he vowed, "I will build a city—my city!" Then and there he resolved to call it Middlesborough.

Arthur dashed back to the headquarters of the railroad company at Newport, Tennessee, only to discover that the Richmond & Danville's directors had voted to merge into a larger line, the East Tennessee, Virginia & Georgia, and that the reconstituted board had no interest in the project. Frustrated but undaunted, he resigned his position with the timber company and caught a train to Asheville. Idle scions of some of the richest families in America loitered there, and Arthur hoped that, through them, he could enlist the financial backing of their parents and of New York and Boston bankers. He sought out a group that included J. H. Martin, Edward Herrick, James Randolph, John Barnard, and F. Randolph Curtis.

Fascinated by Arthur's story and by the bits of coal and iron he had brought back from his journey, nearly a dozen adventurers set out with him to see for themselves. By train and horseback they toiled to the historic notch, set up their tents, and prepared for sleep. Their foray to Arthur's promised land was an exciting one because suddenly—on August 30, 1886—the honeycombed mountain beneath them was shaken by an earthquake. They clung to the quivering earth and listened with awe as boulders crashed down the timbered slopes.[5]

His companions absorbed Arthur's optimism in full, and the scheme grew mightily. Lingering long enough to secure from the disbelieving mountaineers written options on more than 20,000 acres of land, they returned to Asheville with these documents and a couple of bushels of coal and iron specimens. Lawyers drafted articles of incorporation for a company called the Gap Associates, Inc., to which they assigned the options.

While everything had moved splendidly thus far, it suddenly dawned on these budding moguls that their cautious parents were wholly unlikely to sink millions of dollars into a brand-new town in a distant wilderness, and then to spend additional millions to build a railroad to it. Arthur, the dreamer and salesman, quickly devised an escape from their dilemma: he had friends in England and Scotland who would fund the mighty enterprise, if only he could finance a trip to their offices. The "associates" promptly wrote checks, and within days Arthur was aboard a liner bound for England, his precious lumps of coal and iron reposing in a special suitcase.

Arthur's powers of persuasion did not forsake him when he reached London; indeed, he waxed lyrical in the ornate paneled offices of bankers and steel tycoons. His spiel carried the ring of complete plausibility. English financial interests had invested heavily in American railroads, lumber companies, and steel developments. The steel operations at Birmingham, Alabama, were booming, sending back heady returns on both bonds and stocks. Why not invest in another sure thing in the States? The blooming Yanks were bounders, of course—but by Jove, there were ways to make money over there!

Within weeks—nay, days—learned counsel set to work on the formation of a new corporation, the American Association, Ltd., while geologists and mining experts sped across the Atlantic and to the Gap. Their reports to the English moguls confirmed Arthur's glowing rhetoric, and sale of stock in the company began. Sensing something afoot, friends of the organizers clamored for an opportunity to participate, and ample funding was assured. Because the psychology that gives rise to a boom feeds on itself, when Arthur arrived back in America he possessed the virtual equivalent of a blank check. He could build his magic city and all the gigantic enterprises in coal, steel, and lumber that were to sustain it.

Arthur was elected president and general manager of the enterprise. One of his assistants was youthful Otway Cuffe, who in later years would be Sir Otway Fortescue Luke Wheeler Cuffe, Third Baronet of Lyrath, Kilkenny. (After assisting Arthur at Middlesborough, he would go on to greater things as an aide-de-camp to two viceroys in India.) General W. W. Hayward and Colonel Arthur C. Chester Master also assisted Arthur, at a somewhat less lofty level.

The Colson family had owned most of the Middlesborough basin for four generations, living as "land poor" farmers; their house, built of handmade bricks, was regarded as a mansion by neighbors and passersby. Suddenly they were poor no more: the brothers Gilbert, John, and David, and their neighbors and relatives, the Morrisons, sold the Association practically the entire valley. Agents fanned outward to buy additional land in Kentucky, Tennessee, and Virginia. In a trice nearly 100,000 acres were optioned, surveyed, and purchased. The empire builders had gotten up a full head of steam and were plowing through all impediments toward fame, achievement, and fortune.[6]

To keep down costs, Arthur usually employed county-seat lawyers and politicians to buy up needed coal and iron properties. Sometimes, however, he dealt with a landowner directly, especially where a mountaineer was satisfied with his situation and did not want to sell. Since Kentuckians had profound respect for military titles, he assumed the rank of "Captain"; finding this too modest, he elevated himself to "Colonel." After due (but brief) consideration he became "General," and by this august title he was addressed throughout his years at Cumberland Gap.

Determined to avoid the qualms of railroad executives, Arthur let a contract for construction of a tunnel through Cumberland Mountain beneath the Wilderness Road. Simultaneously he set contract builders to work on sixty-five miles of railroad from Knoxville which would connect with the tunnel. Not content with these immense undertakings, he commenced work on a belt line to run around the entire inner perimeter of the valley, with spurs into coves where rich coal veins lay. Determined to promote his new city at all costs, he gave it higher priority than the coal tipples and blast furnaces for which this fantastic enterprise had been conceived.[7]

It must be remembered that the valley was populated only by a handful of families, and that nearly half the land was still covered by huge trees. The nearest railroad was thirteen miles away, a single-track affair designed to transport modest shipments of coal and timber. There were no skilled workmen, no housing for them, no cook houses, hospitals, stores, physicians, dentists, or banks. With supreme confidence that all these lacks could be overcome, Arthur strode in like a titan, directing, assuring, cajoling, and inspiring.

Hundreds of canvas tents were set up in ranks along thoroughfares newly cleared of trees. A multitude of mountaineers used their mules and oxen to drag supplies and building materials to the valley. A few frame houses were erected for Arthur and his aides. Imported physicians set up shop in tents. Sheds were built for cooks, and temporary warehouses held the stores of food. Recruitment efforts had set a horde of people in motion, all of them headed for this new land of promise. In from Kentucky, Tennessee, Alabama, Georgia, and Virginia trooped the hill people, joined by throngs from northern cities and not a few from Great Britain. They embodied every craft and calling, and the labor agents worked frantically to assign workers to appropriate foremen and work gangs. From the Gap the valley appeared to have been occupied by an army of extremely diligent soldiers.

Several hundred men were set to work digging a new channel for Yellow Creek. Since time immemorial it had meandered its crooked way across the valley, but now Colonel George Waring, an engineer from the Empire State, directed an army of men with picks, shovels, drills, and mule-drawn scrapers, setting the stream within straight confines.

Trainloads of imported mules dragged scrapers to level scores of acres for homes and other buildings. Streets were surveyed and paved. New sawmills ripped logs into planks which kilns quickly seasoned. Italian and Hungarian stonecutters carved out blocks of sandstone for foundations and walls. The whine of hand saws and the thump of hammers heralded entire rows of buildings under construction. No expense was spared, and only the ablest engineers and architects were consulted. The town that emerged from the clangor and confusion—from the heaps of bricks and roof tiles, the stacks of lumber, and the welter of sweating men and animals—was a superb expression of the Gay Nineties. In stone and brick and steel, it rose as a product of the Victorian Age—splendid, enduring, and absurd.

Socially the town was a disaster. The weak county government could do nothing to police the community or to punish any but the most blatant criminal acts. Men went armed with pistols, knives, and deadly "slungshots," defending themselves in frequently homicidal gun and knife duels. Whiskey was nearly as common as drinking water. Whores materialized and operated in every imaginable place "beyond company property." Few teetotalers or celibates participated in the building of this costly new town.

In winter, workmen shivered in tents heated only by kerosene lamps. Black cooks from Tennessee served up huge meals which Southerners found tasty but which Northerners eschewed. Fights broke out regularly in the "grub lines" as men squabbled about the food or about their proper places in the long queues. Patent medicine vendors sold cures for colds, piles, rheumatism, constipation, and "bilious stomach." Loan sharks lent small sums at high interest. Con artists moved in to sell shares in even greater projects planned for valleys in other counties. Skillful card players fleeced the unskilled—and were sometimes shot because of it.

Among the toilers were a gaggle of fancily dressed young men from England's most privileged classes. Some sought places for shops, banks, insurance agencies, and other businesses; others were simply spectators who had come to look things over on behalf of their parents. (One such mogul was N. Storey Maskeleyne, a member of Parliament who wanted to "rough it" a while and see what the "chaps were up to.") So outlandish was the situation that teamsters and masons ignored strolling fops attired in silk hats, morning coats, spats, and monocles and brandishing gold-headed walking canes. One youth bought himself a farm, brought in cows, and sold milk, all the while dressed in garments designed for Hyde Park.[8]

Order slowly emerged from the sprawl. Test mines were driven into the hills, and tipples towered above new rail sidings. The tunnel through Cumberland Mountain was finished, and the Louisville & Nashville's line came in from Pineville. The main street—wide and straight, proudly called Cumberland Avenue —was paved with concrete and lined with stores and office buildings for ten blocks. Side streets were going in with similar buildings to front upon them. The most important structures were made of brick and stone with impressive arches, turrets, and gables; two stories were the rule, but a few reached three, plus full basements. Although the rest were built of wood, they were not the flimsy, ramshackle affairs common to frontier towns. Rather, they were made of hardwood, sound weather-boarding on frames fashioned of mortised oak beams, with carved decorations and coats of fresh paint.

As the town went, so did the price of lots. Sales were bois-terous as the bidding escalated to unbelievable levels—in many instances several thousand dollars for a scanty rectangle far from the urban center. People poured in from far and near to capture a spot in this new Eden. Since prevailing wisdom held that values would go upward in perpetuity, buyers felt justified in paying any price.[9]

Every six months Arthur made a hasty trip to London to re-port on his progress and to make sure the money supply was unthreatened. His presentations brought murmurs of pleasure and pledges of more funds as needed. To supplement the flow from London, Arthur reached out to tap the wallets of Ameri-cans. He ordered a custom-built railroad car equipped with dis-play tables and cases, its decorative panels made of twenty-seven woods native to the Tennessee, Virginia, and Kentucky hills. The tables and cases contained fifty-five blocks of hard and soft lumber, plus dozens of specimens of Middlesborough coal, coke, iron, and limestone. Arthur's spieler showed prospective investors a magic-lantern slide show of 200 photographs. Money flowed in for new companies to supply the town with such necessities as gas, water, and electricity.

By the time his forty-fifth birthday rolled around, Arthur had invested four years of his life in the town, which had grown to occupy half the valley. He spent long days of inspection in the saddle, and he worked in his office at the spanking new Middlesborough Hotel. He was tireless, beginning his day at dawn with dictation to a pair of secretaries. He seldom found time to prepare his semi-annual reports to the corporation until he boarded the ship for his voyages to London. These trips generally lasted six weeks.

The Association's board of directors gleamed with gilded names. The chairman, Edmund A. Pontifex, a prominent banking figure, sat on numerous corporate boards and carried the nickname "Guinea" Pontifex because he insisted on receiving that coin for each meeting he attended. The secretary was C. Barclay Holland, son of a director of the Bank of England. Both of these worthies sat also as directors of a subsidiary, Middlesborough Town Land Company, which laid out and sold lots to developers. With such staunch financiers as these to lend credibility to the huge project, the companies never wanted for money. Both were listed on the London Stock Exchange, and dealing in their shares was brisk. Their bonds were gilt edged. The world-famous Baring Brothers Bank extended a generous line of credit. Arthur's accounts were always in order, and there is every reason to believe that he was perfectly honest. Under such circumstances harmony prevailed and work continued almost around the clock.

The Middlesborough Hotel became the town's social center with dances, formal balls, and trysts. In the ornate lobby countless deals were discussed and consummated, and countless bottles of champagne were quaffed. (There, too, a young nobleman got drunk and made a loud and fiery marriage proposal to an indignant black serving maid. When word of this escapade reached his parents, he was summoned home and set to work in less stimulating surroundings.[10])

But the moguls did not advance without setbacks. On a bright May morning in 1890, a spectacular fire broke out and spread swiftly, consuming more than half the town. Looting began, and the rest was saved only by speedy action to destroy the stocks of whiskey that merchants had carried onto the streets.

Letcher County Court House, ca. 1890, when large-scale buying of minerals was under way. (Alice Lloyd College Archives, Pippa Passes, Ky.)

County Store and some of its patrons, Rock House Creek, Letcher County, 1884. (Alice Lloyd College Archives.)

Widow and children of Henry Morris at their home on Looney Creek, Harlan County, 1903. Lynch was later built on this land. (Alice Lloyd College Archives.)

Building of Middlesborough, ca. 1888. All of these buildings were destroyed by the first fire. (Source unknown.)

Lot auction at Middlesborough during the Big Boom. The old city hall is shown in the background. (Source unknown.)

Booneway Hotel, Middlesborough, with electric railway in foreground, 1890. (Source unknown.)

The Middlesborough Hotel survived, but most of the wooden structures and some of the better stores, office buildings, and homes lay in ashes.[11] With the conflagration the boom flickered. The new municipal corporation was left with a debt of $150,000 which had been incurred for the waterworks, sewage plant, and street lights.

Although the town was bankrupt, hope was not abandoned. A slate of inventive officials were elected, reforms were instituted, and "economy" became the town's unofficial slogan. At Arthur's urging, the company provided loans to enable people ruined by the catastrophe to rebuild. Most did so, and within little more than a year all but a few of the fire-cleared lots had been filled with new stone and brick structures. Anyone who expressed a doubt about the eternal nature of the boom was castigated by all and sundry as a "knocker," a "stumbling block," a "sorehead" or, infinitely worse, as lacking patriotism and true faith in God.

The indefatigable Arthur simultaneously built Harrogate near the state line in Tennessee. Also named for a town in England, it was designed as a distant and detached suburb of Middlesborough—an exclusive neighborhood where fatigued moguls could take respite in spacious mansions set amid extensive grounds. Here life would be lived as in English country houses—in elegance and quiet, attended always by proper English servants.[12]

On a hill at Harrogate architects set the crown jewel of the whole vast work. For a million dollars (a fantastic sum) the breathtaking Four Seasons Hotel was constructed. Seen from a distance across the even bluegrass sward, it floated like a stupendous Turkish palace, occupying most of the farm where Dr. Harbison had entertained Arthur on his first trip to the Gap. Arthur had convinced two prominent New York physicians, Dr. Allan McLane Hamilton and Dr. Holbrook Curtis, to build the monstrosity. (Dr. Curtis was a brother of one of the "Gap Associates" at Asheville.) Arthur had assured them that sparkling mountain water and the clean, bracing air would restore health to their ailing patients. Mineral springs were located, and construction of the gigantic spa was undertaken with the same frenetic energy that Arthur had aroused at Middlesborough. New York investors provided funds to build it and $500,000 more to furnish it.

Completed in 1892, the Four Seasons Hotel was such a work as Tennessee is not likely to see again. The immense white four-story hostelry contained 700 rooms and absorbed 200 boxcar loads of windows and doors. The silverware, china, beds, and other furnishings were of the highest quality. Riding trails, strolling paths, tennis courts, golf links, shuffleboards, card rooms, and an almost endless line of rocking chairs offered relaxation and solace to the well and the sick. A 200-room sanitorium with elaborate Turkish baths sheltered the latter. A carriage road was cut into the mountains so that convalescents could be carried comfortably to the scenic heights.

When the Four Seasons opened in the spring of 1892, New York's "Four Hundred" social elite arrived in a chartered express train. At the grand ball they were attended by a carefully selected staff of 150 chefs, waiters, maids, porters, and valets. The pilgrimage was headed by Mrs. Paran Stevens, the wife of Manhattan's leading hotel tycoon.[13]

Harrogate and Middlesborough were visited by London brokers who dealt in shares of the companies, and the frenzied construction encouraged them to tout the stocks. In 1891 the Duke and Duchess of Marlboro came to see what was going on, followed in due time by Viscount James Bryce. Bryce was a former ambassador to Washington, and both he and the Duke expressed confidence in the way their funds were being expended. The Earl of Dysart spent several days with Arthur. All thought it was a grand thing to see British money at work in the Appalachian backwoods.

While these affairs were underway, Arthur was not devoting quite all his time to the company. He found interludes during which to build himself a magnificent home on a part of the old Harbison farm, which by then had been wholly consumed by the Four Seasons and by spacious residential lots. There he planned to live out his days in service to the American Association and the new Pittsburgh.

Middlesborough had grown from a few derelict farms in a strange round valley to a city of at least five thousand. Its straight, spacious avenues were laid out as if in anticipation of the automobile age. By 1890 there were built or under construction five churches, an iron furnace, a tannery, a city hall and court house, two imposing school buildings, an opera house, an immense hotel-casino, a Carnegie library, a newspaper, a brewery, an ice house, a hospital, numerous office buildings, sixteen hotels, four banks, and rows of huge, comfortable houses. Eighty stores and other businesses opened onto concrete walks and streets; seventy others were planned. All the structures were solid and imposing. Even the dozens of "tenant houses" were of an extraordinary quality for the time. From property line to property line Cumberland Avenue, the rip-roaring main street, was one hundred feet wide. The lesser streets measured a mere eighty feet.[14]

The mighty development effort sent more than $30 million into the backwoods El Dorado at the Kentucky and Tennessee line, a sum that would exceed $600 million in today's depreciated currency. In addition, there was the cost of the railroad leading to the new Mecca, plus its huge tunnel and its prim valley beltline.

Alexander Alan Arthur and his English friends had built well; unfortunately, they had not built wisely, as scores of ruined investors would soon attest. Their economic bubble collapsed, even as the Four Seasons was being built. Arthur was discharged as president of the American Association on January 12, 1891. When the glittering hotel opened to receive New York's Four Hundred, Arthur was fighting for survival.

In November, 1890, the Baring Brothers Bank closed its doors. It had extended enormous credit on the most tenuous security, and its failure set off a panic with grave repercussions throughout England. Some of Arthur's major backers were bankrupted and many others were seriously weakened. Worried, Arthur rushed to London for consultations. Additional millions would be required to put the iron and coal works into profitable operation, and he learned immediately that such funding could not be expected. Interest on the corporation's bonded indebtedness was coming due to English investors, and the money, instead of being invested in profit-making developments, had gone into construction of a gleaming city. The mighty tunnel was complete, but the ironworks and coal mines could not be profitably operated because costly work remained to be done on the railroad. Under these circumstances the bond coupons failed of redemption. The American Association's stock plummeted from £40 to £1.5. Arthur was absolved of wrongdoing, but he was finished as president and general manager. Director E. F. Powers was designated to succeed him.

When Arthur arrived back in Middlesborough in the spring of 1891, he was greeted as a hero. The people who had invested in the new town—in its lots, shops, and buildings—could not bring themselves to believe that the boom would not go on. It had all been so marvelous, so dizzying in its climb that the psychology of boom had become as vital as their heartbeat. Arthur had caused the good times; without him, Middlesborough would have been a weed-grown pasture. Moved by precisely the same impulse, Powers investigated the huge project and found it essentially sound. He notified the directors that their investments were secure. He thought, however, that there had been "a little too much booming," and that more cautious policies should be followed in the future.

But funds from England could no longer be relied on. For a time the "boomers" lived on their optimism, their dogged faith that the great times could not die. They reassured one another and prospective investors elsewhere that nothing really had changed. So effective were they at convincing themselves that a total of $350,000 was taken in at a lot sale held on May 1, 1891. Mrs. Alexander Arthur bought a prime corner lot for $410 per front foot—$41,000!

The town's troubles had begun with that visit by the Duke and Duchess of Marlboro. Though the jovial Duke entertained Arthur and dubbed him "Duke of Middlesborough," he saw much more than he let on. In a letter to the directors he laid his finger on the corporation's real difficulty:

> Over four millions sterling has been spent on the development of the property. . . . So far it has all been money going out; and, moreover, the sales of land in shares that have brought in ready money only represent . . . the confidence of investors in the future of the place and the prospective worth of town lots. The real test must come in the success of the basic steel process. . . . I

would rather wait and see what was the output of the two large sets of furnaces . . . before I could feel assured that the scale of prices that is being paid for town lots is justified.[15]

When the iron ore that Arthur had prospected south of the Gap was re-assayed by other geologists, their findings were enough to chill the blood. Iron was there, but the deposits were not large. The ore ledges were thinner than had been previously supposed, and the quality was mediocre—much inferior to that found in Alabama.

While the gargantuan Four Seasons was rising at Harrogate, Middlesborough began to sink. One by one, construction projects slowed or ground to a halt. The factories that were to provide the city's economic diversity appeared, in a new light, as preposterous white elephants. The tannery, the brewery, the steel mill and its furnaces, the immense ice house—all suddenly loomed up, overbuilt and unsustainable. Where would the hides be found for the tannery? How would this wilderness provide the host of drinkers to keep that imposing brewery at work? How could the furnaces and forge be fed from those thin ore ledges, and to whom would the iron and steel be sold? Along the new streets and avenues merchants looked at their shelves stocked with shirts, ties, and shoes, and they wondered who would buy. Tailors, dentists, doctors, pharmacists thought about customers and patients. They worried and they began to leave. Expensive lots remained empty. Shop doors were locked and "To Let" signs were hung in windows. The "boomers" fell silent.

The hard times since remembered as the panic of 1893 began to grip America. To the evaporation of English capital was added a full-scale American crash. In this general debacle Middlesborough plunged like a falling star. A community that had been conceived as the capital and center of an immense new industrial empire was left stranded, bereft and unfinished. It sprawled along "avenues" and streets hideous and derelict, forsaken by the workmen and artisans.

The foppish English youths went home. The managers, engineers, architects, and contractors salvaged what little they could. Most of the mountaineers slipped back to their hidden farms in the hills to ponder the strange ways of the educated and wealthy. Most people who remained in the "tenant houses" and in the imposing Victorian mansions and homes were from the hills of the tri-state region; they were lawyers, doctors, and merchants who managed to buy, at insignificant prices, homes and commercial buildings that had been built at great cost. The excitement and activity ebbed, and Middlesborough sank into a slumber—the somnolent successor to the trifling hamlet of Cumberland Gap. Gradually the piles of unused brick, stone, and lumber were sold off. Incomplete buildings stood stark and gloomy until they were demolished for their materials or (in a few cases) until better times brought their completion.

Bankruptcy and liquidation were Middlesborough's major industries in 1893 and 1894. All four of the town's banks collapsed, and depositors and shareholders received nothing. The twenty-seven-mile-long beltline that cost the corporation more than $1 million was sold to the Louisville & Nashville for $30,000. In one year the Town Land Company's assets shrank by more than 90 percent. The American Association, Ltd., vanished with a total loss to every stock and bond holder. The corporation's vast holdings shrank from 150,000 acres to 80,000; then these, too, were auctioned by the county sheriff for $15,000—less than 18 cents per acre! The lands were bought by a new syndicate of the same name and composed of most of the major investors in the original American Association.

The huge plant of Watts Steel & Iron Company, nearly finished when the debacle came, was completed, and it operated two blast furnaces on an irregular and unprofitable basis for four years. The Boston Gun Works expired in 1897.[16] The receivers operated out of the impressive buildings of the defunct Coal & Iron Bank. The dead companies covered a wide range— banks, steel, coal, coke, coffins, waterworks, breweries, insurance, retail shops, hostelries, restaurants, wholesale groceries, brickyards, lumber, and lime.

Saddest of all was the shambling demise of that pathetic giant, the Four Seasons Hotel. Three years after its grand opening and gala ball, it was sold to the Chicago Wrecking and Salvage Company for $9,000—nine-tenths of 1 percent of its cost. The sanitorium was left to rot, its paint peeling, its hundreds of windowpanes caked with dirt.[17]

Churches and a couple of private schools shared in the ignominious plunge. The shrunken congregations gathered in tabernacles built to shelter large flocks of Methodists, Baptists, Presbyterians, and Disciples of Christ. Tiny classes studied in a few rooms of buildings designed for hordes of children. But the English imprint remained in the imposing walls, towers, turrets, arches, and architraves. It persisted also in the cemetery where a few Englishmen were buried, probably because they were too poor to go home. Young Valentine Blake, son of Sir Valentine Blake of Menlough Castle, Ireland, is there, as is Colonel Arthur C. Chester Master, Alexander Arthur's old aide and confidant.

As a community, as a city, as an organized concept, and as an architectural accomplishment, Middlesborough was a success.[18] Its valley is spacious and the mountains that tower above it are lovely, but they stand at enough distance that they do not overpower and crush the psyche. The broad streets and ample lots add to the feeling of spaciousness. The sturdy buildings lend an air of permanence, a quality so lacking in most coal-country towns. Arthur and his colleagues left behind more than mortar, bricks, and roof tiles; their work is an island of refinement and inspiration.[19]

Arthur tried to rebuild his life, but nothing ever worked out for him again. His vast energy had ebbed, and with it had gone his incredible power to inspire, lead, and persuade. At last he came home to die, on March 4, 1912. His grave, only a few yards from David Colson's, overlooks what is left of Boone's trace, the Wilderness Road, the once-busy hog road with its herds of grunting swine. The place is as silent now as when he spent that fateful night with Dr. Harbison. If there are ghosts, we may suppose that the wraith of Alexander Alan Arthur walks the old road by midnight to visit his peaceful town.

Despite its ill fortune, Middlesborough survived. In time a paved highway was built through the Gap to link Kentucky to Tennessee and Virginia, and the road brought visitors. The community was a pleasant place in which to live, and affluent coal operators sought it out for retirement. A federal park was established to commemorate the historic pass, and tourists spend dollars along the tranquil streets. The name was shortened to Middlesboro; the pace slowed to a modest walk, and life goes on. While the proud boast of the boomers that the new city of Cumberland Gap would become the home of 150,000 Americans was never achieved, there has been growth, and today a tenth of that number may live in the valley. Middlesboro's golf course is among the oldest in the United States, and the little municipal electric plant found new customers, grew, and became a giant—the Kentucky Utilities Company.

Eastern Kentucky's first boom had come and gone, but elsewhere other moguls dreamed of empires in the hills. The spectacular developments at Cumberland Gap set off an explosion in other parts of the Appalachians. Inspired by "the Pittsburgh of the South," a mania for the building of coal and iron towns swept through neighboring states between 1889 and 1893. The region was liberally sprinkled with "new cities": Norton, Appalachia, and Big Stone Gap in Virginia; Meeksborough, Tennessee; Tallapoosa, Georgia; Florence, Alabama. Without exception these "boomer cities" collapsed during or soon after 1893 amid bickering, name-calling, bankruptcies, and a few vengeance shootings. The saddest of them all was the now nearly vanished town of Arthur, Tennessee, whose promoters had grandiloquently named it for the greatest boomer of them all.[20]

At the Gap, capitalism had gone berserk. Thousands of people went quite mad, flinging their savings and hopes into a wild mountainous backwoods, gambling that coal and steel would boom forever. The towns they built memorialize the inevitability of the business cycle, the inexorable sequence of boom and bust.

In the 1960's the American Association made news in England, when a reporter for the *Manchester Guardian* disclosed that the company was pursuing strip-mining procedures that were destroying mountains, devastating forests, and filling streams with mud.[21] Accustomed to such environmental ravages, Americans were quite unimpressed, but the outrage aroused in Great Britain was considerable. At that time the chairman was a quaintly named money baron, Sir Denys Flowerdew Lowson, who was also lord mayor of the venerable City of London. At his death a decade later, the net worth of Lowson's estate exceeded £200 million. His attitude toward the Americans who lived on and around his corporation's land was as contemptuous as that expressed in 1882 by the lordly railroad tycoon William Henry Vanderbilt: "The public be damned!" Lowson's international business practices on three continents never departed perceptibly from that Vanderbilt precept. Where his predecessors experienced disappointment and impoverishment, Lowson found vast wealth in exploiting the land and people in and around the "magic city." But that is a story in and of itself.[22]

THREE

The First Moguls

THE STORY OF THE FORTUNES and personalities that industrialized the Kentucky hills reaches back to a coal field east of the Alleghenies when the age of steam was born. Eastern moguls and their sons were pioneers in a new world of coal, steam, railroads, steel, and petroleum, and they blazed their trail through it as confidently as Boone and his men had carved a way through Cumberland Gap. Their pioneering efforts established precedents that were, in due time, applied to Kentucky; when the process was complete, there would be railroad tracks where only dim mule paths had run. The map would be sprinkled with the names of grand new aristocrats: Jenkins, McRoberts, Hemphill, Haymond, Fleming, Wayland, Van Lear, Weeksbury, Garrett, Hellier, and Warfield. Their ordered rows of houses, their stores and warehouses, their power plants, icehouses, machine shops, tipples, and mines would transform three entire valleys. Men would name their sons for the moguls, and mountain mothers would look at their comely daughters and hope that they would catch the approving eyes of the sons of the "big bosses."

The juggernaut that would overwhelm Kentucky was born in Maryland. The Appalachian mineral fields have been called an economic colony owned and governed for the profit of eastern banks, corporations, and tax-exempt foundations.[1] The capture of Appalachia and the rendering out of its wealth for the benefit of absentee owners began in the coal-rich hills and valleys of Maryland's Allegany County. The exploiters were an uncommon lot of suave New Englanders whose ancestors had long been prominent in national affairs and whose descendants would continue the tradition.

Maryland's western neck is a triangular expanse of broken land that includes the valley of George's Creek, flowing between Dan's Mountain on the east and Big Savage Mountain and Little Savage Mountain to the west. By 1750 perceptive pioneers had detected coal in the hillsides, and in the late 1700's it was being mined for use by blacksmiths. After 1800 a trade grew up in which the fuel was dug from "coal banks" and floated in clumsy wooden barges down to Georgetown and other markets along the Potomac.

In 1828 work began on the Chesapeake & Ohio Canal, giving promise of efficient transportation of George's Creek coal to Baltimore and the coastal market. This event inspired a small band of entrepreneurs to organize the Maryland Mining Company, an ambitious enterprise capitalized at $200,000 and authorized to own 5,000 acres of land.[2]

Even more pretentious than the beginning of work on the canal was the incorporation, in that same year, of America's first railroad, the Baltimore & Ohio. When completed, the 184-mile-long canal was reliable for only part of the year. In the winter it was often frozen solid or blocked by ice jams. At other times the water was low, or too much traffic caused obstructions and delays. But the railroad—on which work began only three years after the world's first, the Stockton & Darlington in England, demonstrated that steel rails and steam engines could beat mules, wagons, and canal boats—wrought the real revolution. Steam and rails made coal available in competition with firewood, created markets for still more coal, and stimulated the opening of mines farther west in Pennsylvania and West Virginia. This grandfather of American railroads would roll triumphantly across the West Virginia hills and up the Big Sandy Valley until it reached Jenkins, Kentucky, on the upper reaches of Elkhorn Creek in 1911.[3]

Mining methods were extremely primitive when steam transportation set off the modern industrial age in America. Tunnels were driven straight back into the hillside coal veins; then lateral tunnels were turned off from the main headings. This "tunnel and pillar" mining proceeded until the weak ventilation system could no longer propel air to the "working face," a place of hard labor and terrible danger. The whole operation was done by hand, in a process that killed or wore out countless workmen. Oak timbers held up the overhead ledge of slate and sandstone, while miners used sharp-pointed picks to dig out a band of coal about two feet thick extending along the floor the width of the tunnel. The same tools were used to hack out a similar segment next to the "rib" on each side; then steel wedges were driven into the coal where it joined the top, and by this means a huge block was wedged loose. After it dropped to the floor it was attacked with picks, sledgehammers, and wedges and split into manageable lumps. These were shoveled into "bank cars" and pushed by men or drawn by mules to the tipping horns (or tipple) outside the entry (or driftmouth).

These simple procedures required legions of laborers. Because the work was in remote and sparsely populated mountainous districts, the employers had to build houses to shelter the laborers and stores to sell them necessities. The communities were flimsily built for transient populations who would leave when the coal vein played out, or when the workings extended so far underground that they had to be abandoned. The first coal camps grew up in the valleys east of "the western waters." The essential relationships between the mining companies and miners were established here, in the primitive communities built by these budding antebellum moguls.[4]

Frostburg and Lonaconing became the centers of this growing coal industry. New companies were chartered to build camps and open mines on Jennings Run, George's Creek, and their tributary streams. The coal ranged from six to eleven feet in thickness and was of excellent quality. As the demand for it grew in industries and on household hearths, the mines multiplied. English capital financed the George's Creek Coal & Iron Company in 1835. In 1837 Englishmen bought stock subscriptions of £120,000 in the Maryland & New York Iron & Coal Company. When the railroad reached the valley, twelve companies held charters for mining, and four already had installations ready to produce.

With the Civil War, coal boomed, and during the Gilded Age

that followed it branch rail lines were extended up the tributaries to new camps and tipples. During the war coal-fired furnaces produced iron for cannons, warships, and a million rifles. Then came the transcontinental railroad and the steel-frame skycraper, the steel "tin can," and eventually the automobile. New investors headed for the Maryland coal fields to obtain what is called, in modern parlance, a "position in coal."

The Borden Mining Company, for example, drew its capital from Massachusetts, primarily from investors in Fall River. The Borden family controlled a textile mill, a company that manufactured and sold heating gas, and a railroad that ran down to Boston.[5] Edward Cunard, founder of the Cunard steamship line, and August Belmont, banker and mining tycoon, incorporated the Lonaconing Ocean Coal Mining & Transportation Company in 1853. Their firm gulped George's Creek coal as steamships drove the clippers from the seas.

The scope of the boom is shown by the valley's shipments in 1853. The canal transported 83,000 tons, and the Baltimore & Ohio carried out another 175,000 tons.[6]

In that year Warren Delano appeared in the Maryland field—a striking figure who would play a major role in opening the Appalachian fields farther west. Born at Fairhaven, Massachusetts, in 1809, he was of old New England stock. (His family was originally deLannoye, and his first ancestor had reached Plymouth in 1621.) After studying in private academies and spending an interlude in a Boston bank, he went to China in 1834 as a supercargo for John Murray Forbes of Boston. He remained in China for nine years and, upon his return, went into the mercantile business in New York. He accumulated a substantial fortune and sired eleven children, one of whom, Sara, married James Roosevelt and became the mother of Franklin Delano Roosevelt.[7]

John Murray Forbes had roots deep in Maryland coal. He and Erastus Corning (a New York railroad tycoon) and John F. Winslow (a fellow Bostonian) formed the Mt. Savage Iron Work in 1843. Their iron deposit soon played out, but the syndicate was left with sizable coal holdings. These Mt. Savage mining operations were probably the first "captive" mines in the United States. Delano came to George's Creek to help organize a new railroad, the Cumberland & Pennsylvania. The subscription books were opened on April 15, 1853, and the first board of directors included Forbes, Delano, and John F. Winslow.

William Aspinwall was a founder of the Pacific Mail Steamship Company and of the Panama Isthmus Railroad. He was a brother of Sara Roosevelt's mother—hence Warren Delano's brother-in-law. His steamers burned Maryland coal and he had a keen interest in the region's developing industries. He owned several thousand acres of "big vein" coal and was president of the Ocean Steam Coal Company.[8] In 1860 Aspinwall took the lead in forming a new company which sought for coal the benefits that John D. Rockefeller, Sr., would later secure for oil. He persuaded most of the valley's coal companies to merge their operations into a new conglomerate, the Consolidation Coal Company, which survives today as the nation's second-largest (in some years, the largest) coal producer. The Civil War delayed the company's completion, and it was not formally organized until April 19, 1864. Its first directors included Corning, Forbes, and Aspinwall. Later in the year Delano was elected to the board; he was joined by his son-in-law, James Roosevelt, in 1868. Harry Crawford Black came out from Baltimore to look over his family's substantial investments, merged them into Consolidation, and in due time became a director.[9]

With the formation of Consolidation Coal, the industry took on a new and cohesive form. Less time would be devoted to competition and more to organization and planning. With their operations based on the superb coals of western Maryland, the moguls were assured of markets. Their investments in railroads and steamship lines promised efficient delivery to foreign and domestic consumers. The infant industry, now consolidated and under the leadership of men with broad national and international perspectives, could plan terminals and docks on the oceans and the Great Lakes, and could envision profitable involvement in chemicals and steel. The new company's link to the big banks assured necessary funding as further opportunities might arise. The moguls could look forward to the Golden Age of Coal.

At least some of these urbane figures deserve a closer look. They were older than the predators who came to power and wealth with Rockefeller and who applied his cold and mechanical methods in order to pile up money. They were better educated in the formal sense, more widely traveled, and somewhat more tolerant of the legitimate needs of others. This is not to intimate that they approved of such vexatious innovations as labor unions, but they did tend to see the need for publicly financed education as a tool for social uplift. They were conservative, but scarcely akin to the Neanderthals who would succeed them on King Coal's throne.

John Murray Forbes is illustrative. Born in France in 1813 while his parents were there on business, he grew up in Massachusetts and was educated at the Franklin Academy, at Andover, and at Joseph Cogswell's school in Northampton. At 13 he entered the business world as a clerk in a company engaged in the China spice, silk, and porcelain trade. In 1830 Forbes went to China to represent the company. Because of his sagacious dealings with the Chinese he was made a full partner in 1834. One Mandarin official was so impressed that he placed a half-million dollars in Forbes's hands for investment in U.S. properties. In China Forbes became an agent of the Baring Brothers Bank. He came back to Boston and,' at the age of twenty-six, established J. M. Forbes & Co., a shipping and mercantile firm. Forbes built up a fleet of the lean clipper ships that were revolutionizing world trade; simultaneously he took an interest in the evolving railroads, particularly the Michigan Central. He assembled a syndicate and bought the line, then extended its tracks from Kalamazoo to Chicago, Detroit, and Buffalo. He branched out into other lines and formed the railroads that became the Chicago, Burlington & Quincy. He remained active in the building of mid-continent railroads, and in coal and steel, until his death in 1898.

Forbes was a Massachusetts Republican elector in 1861. He was a friend and confidant of President Lincoln, who sent him and William Aspinwall to England in a futile attempt to buy a number of speedy steam-powered raiders then under construction for the Confederate Navy. Although the emissaries could not obtain the vessels, they took time to negotiate a much-needed $2,500,000 loan from the Baring Brothers Bank to the United States Treasury.

Forbes often counseled with his close friend William Cullen

Bryant, editor of the *New York Post*, and entertained at his home such figures as Grover Cleveland, Charles Francis Adams, Wendell Phillips, John Greenleaf Whittier, and Ralph Waldo Emerson. He was one of the most influential Americans of his time in several fields: politics, economics, trade, finance, and letters. (His daughter published his *Letters and Recollections* in two volumes a few years after he died.) With such a background it is easy to sense his power in the Maryland west when the American coal industry was being given its basic shape and direction.[10]

Forbes's friend, James Roosevelt, was born to the purple at Hyde Park when the eighteen-year-old was already in China. Claes Martenzen Van Roosevelt had come to New York in 1649. He was the ancestor not only of James Roosevelt, but also of two presidents of the United States. James's mother was Mary Rebecca Aspinwall, and through her he was linked by blood to his fellow mogul, William Aspinwall. Roosevelt graduated from Harvard in 1851 and practiced law in New York for a few years. Aspinwall interested him in the coal industry, and this led to investment in a half-dozen railroads and a seat on the board of Consolidation Coal.

James Roosevelt's directorships sound like a roll call of the major enterprises that were forging industrial America in the last half of the nineteenth century: railroads, steamboats, canals (including one in Nicaragua), banks, trust companies, coal, and the first holding company of its kind, the Southern Railway Security Company. He served on an impressive list of philanthropic boards and agencies and belonged to the most prestigious clubs: the Holland Society, Delta Phi fraternity, and the Metropolitan Clubs of New York and Washington. His photograph reveals a mutton-chopped face full of poise, self-assurance, and calm. It is the face of a man perfectly capable of siring and raising America's most consummate politician and the only president to be elected more than twice, all the while building a vast industrial country for this extraordinary son to govern.[11]

These masters of a fast-growing industry were aided by Robert Garrett, a prominent merchant-banker of Baltimore. His Savings Bank of Baltimore financed some of Aspinwall's biggest steamships. His younger kinsman of the same name became a director of the Baltimore & Ohio Railroad, and the three banks which he served as a director put large sums into the company's extensions into eastern Kentucky after 1900. His corporate and philanthropic directorships marked him as a member of the power elite.[12] His fellow moguls named for him the town of Garrett in Floyd County, Kentucky.

Another loyal servant of the moguls was Edwin Warfield, who was elected governor of Maryland in 1903. When labor strife broke out in the coal field, Warfield promptly sent the state militia to restore order. His family, aided by Maryland industrialists, developed huge natural gas holdings in eastern Kentucky in the 1920's. Out of Warfield's line came Wallis Warfield Simpson, whose love affair with an English king compelled him to abdicate the throne in 1936. The name of Warfield, Kentucky, perpetuates the fame of these politicians, industrialists, and bankers.

These first moguls laid the foundations of an immense U.S. coal industry and constructed the rail system to carry it to markets. As the coal and railroad industries grew, their wealth would increase also—as would their quiet, unostentatious power.

What of the men whose sweat and labor enriched these polite, educated, and urbane industrialists and their families? The poet-editor William Cullen Bryant came out to visit one of their mines and left us a rare written insight:

> Our party made a visit to a coal-mine some three miles distant from Mount Savage. From one of the black entrances flowed a lively little stream with yellow waters, into which I dipped my finger to ascertain their flavor. It was acidulous and astringent, holding in solution both alum and copperas. Leaving the Stygian rivulet we came to another entrance, out of which a train of loaded trucks was passing, every one of which was attended by a miner blackened from head to foot with the dust of his task, and wearing in the front a small crooked lamp to light his way. As they emerged from the darkness they looked like sooty demons of the mine with the flaming horns coming from the womb of the mountain. We now entered, each carrying a lantern, attended by a guide. The vein of coal is from eight to ten feet thick, and the

passage is of that height, with a roof of glistening slate, propped in some places by wooden posts.

Here and there, on each side of the passage, yawned chambers cut in the veins of coal, and extending beyond the reach of the eye in the faint light of our lanterns. At length we heard the sound of sledges, and proceeding for some distance farther came to the end of the passage, where the workmen, each with a lamp in his cap, were driving wedges into the cracks and fissures of the coal to separate it from the roof and walls. We saw several large blocks detached in this manner, the workmen jumping aside when they fell, and then we retraced our steps. Before returning to the entrance, however, our guides took us into a branch of the main passage, in which, after proceeding a little way, we heard a roar as of flames, and then we saw a fierce light before us. A furnace appeared, in which a fierce fire was blazing; the blackened workmen were stirring and feeding it, and a strong current of air rushing by us went with the flames up the shaft, which reached above to the surface of the ground. This, we are told, was a contrivance to ventilate the mine. All the foul air and all the fire damp and other noxious gases are drawn up and carried off from the passages and chambers by this method. On our way back to the entrance, we perceived that the veins lay at just such an inclination as allowed the workmen to roll the loaded trucks by hand along an easy descent to the mouth, as I hear is the case with all the mines.[13]

FOUR

The Fairmont Ring

AMONG THE EARLIEST SETTLERS in the Monongahela Valley of West Virginia were William Haymond and two brothers named Joab and Benoni Fleming. For protection against marauding Shawnees they built their hewed log houses near Jacob Prickett's fort. The land was rich, and the community prospered and grew. In 1803, nearly thirty years after the Haymonds and Flemings arrived, James Greene Watson crossed the hills from Maryland with his wife, five children, and slaves. The Haymonds, Flemings, and Watsons intermarried, and their clan increased. Eventually the settlement became the city of Fairmont, and the three families were prominent in the affairs of the upper Monongahela.

They were Democrats. Some were Methodists and the others were Episcopalians; all were conservative in politics but aggressive in business. They farmed, operated grist and saw mills, and acquired huge landholdings. They held numerous state and county offices.

Thomas Watson married Rebecca Haymond and in 1815 their son, James Otis, was born. He grew to sturdy manhood and in 1841 married Matilda Lamb. This young couple set up housekeeping in a log house purchased from Alexander Fleming and eventually had ten children, of whom the youngest was Clarence Wayland Watson.

James Otis Watson was not destined to spend his days in a log house. Plow handles did not fit his huge hands, and he began to ponder the mining activity that had shattered the tranquility of the George's Creek Valley beyond Big Savage Mountain to the east. He went to Maryland and observed the mining operations and installations, and he decided to get into the coal business. Too canny to court the pitfalls that accompany ignorance and inexperience, he enlisted the aid of Neil Gaskill, one of the ablest mining engineers of the time, and in 1852 organized the Montana Mining Company. Watson, "the father of the West Virginia coal industry," was by no means the first to mine coal in the state, but he was the first to ship coal by rail. He and Gaskill systematized coal mining far beyond production procedures followed by the moguls east of the Big Savage.[1]

The building of the Baltimore & Ohio Railroad to the Monongahela and on to Wheeling was an engineering triumph that would not be equaled even in the intricate valleys and mountains of Kentucky. The extension across the steep, rocky slopes of the Alleghenies required 11 tunnels and 113 bridges, one of which was the longest steel span in the United States at the time.[2]

During the next thirty years capital from the banks of Baltimore steadily expanded production in the Fairmont field. The proliferating mines included operations called the Newburg Orrel Coal Company and the American Gas Coal Company. H. Y. Attrill opened a mine and built coke ovens. Aretas Brooks Fleming and James Otis Watson commenced mining at Gaston. The coal towns, following the precedent set for them in Maryland, were entirely self-contained; each hamlet in its hollow consisted of houses, stores, an office for the visiting company doctor, a yawning shaft or two into the cleared hillside, gaunt black tipples, and growing mounds of slate and discarded coal. Wages were abysmally low, and the boundless throngs of native and imported laborers who clamored for jobs kept them from rising. The hill people were oppressed and impoverished by the approaching exhaustion of their land. In addition, huge tracts were being sold off to lumber and coal companies; once the money from the sales slipped away, the former owners were themselves compelled to enter the mines. There were no workmen's compensation laws, and the injured, widowed, and orphaned began accumulating in and around the mining communities. Because West Virginia adhered to the legal doctrine of "assumption of risk," moguls were absolved from liability when roof falls or exploding methane snuffed out lives.[3]

Fairmont, West Virginia, was a small, nondescript city in the last decades of the nineteenth century, but not all its people were commonplace or unknown. Circumstances had met and meshed to create both money and influence, especially in the Watson-Fleming-Haymond circles. Later, when they were joined by Johnson Newlon Camden, Sr., with his Standard Oil millions, the allied families and their associated business and political cohorts became formidable indeed.[4]

The small group of clever politicians who were known in their own state as "the Fairmont ring" moved into the eastern Kentucky coal field, and into the state's political arena, long after they had subjugated West Virginia. Before turning to the legacy of the Fairmont ring, it is important to investigate the West Virginia background of its originators. The sons and heirs of the New Englanders who had earlier moved into western Maryland's Allegany County would accompany the ring, providing it with money and political muscle and sharing fully in the profits. In Kentucky the Fairmonters would be at the forefront, but scions of the older wealth would be their willing abettors at every stage.

The world's first well intended specifically to produce petroleum was drilled near Titusville, Pennsylvania, in 1859. The hole, fifty-nine-and-a-half feet deep, was dug by a wheezing steam-powered rig, and the project required a year to organize and execute. In the context of the times it was a gusher, at twenty-five barrels per day, and with it the Oil Age was born. The drillers worked for Edwin L. Drake, who thought this rock oil or petroleum might be used as an inexpensive substitute for oil distilled from cannel coal and rendered from the fat of whales. The well was on land owned by Brewer, Watson & Company, a timber corporation. One of the owners, Jonah Watson, immediately secured options on several farms, and he soon had a well of his own flowing at the breathtaking rate of sixty barrels per day. The well and two others produced a total of 165,000 barrels, and the petroleum sold for 60 cents per gallon. The future was bright for the Pennsylvania kinsmen of James Otis Watson: he was about to become America's first oil millionaire.[5]

The Civil War presented a thorny problem for the three

closely linked families. As Democrats, they felt sympathy for
Virginia and the South, and they had owned slaves since the first
pioneer settlements. But they were realists, and as 1861 approached their expectations and loyalties shifted to the North.
These industrialists saw that the slave-worked cotton economy
of the Confederacy was doomed in a military contest with the
coal, iron, and steam of the North. Besides, the developing markets of the Monongahela coal basin were in the North, and a
division of the country would subject their products to tariffs at
best and total exclusion from Yankee consumers at worst. Consequently they supported the Lincoln administration, and when
the referendum on the new state of West Virginia came up in
1863, they voted to divide the Old Dominion.

(A respectable body of opinion holds that West Virginia was
created in response to demands of the Baltimore & Ohio Railroad and the growing industrial community in Virginia's western counties. It is pointed out that most West Virginians were
never opposed to slavery, and that its statehood convention sent
Congress a proposed constitution that endorsed and protected
the peculiar institution. Both Lincoln and Congress rejected the
document, and West Virginia entered the union as a reluctant
free state. The B&O's growing empire was reaching out to tap
the commerce of the vast, fertile Ohio Valley, and a Confederate
victory would have been catastrophic to the company's future.)

Peter H. Watson served as assistant secretary of war under the
irascible but competent Edwin Stanton. He became acquainted
with railroad developers and clearly foresaw the importance of
the rails in the inevitable postwar expansion. He cultivated the
tycoons and, after the war, became general freight agent for the
Michigan & Southern Railroad. Among his new friends were
William and John D. Rockefeller, with whom he cooperated in
setting up the rate rebate system that quickly and illegally built
"the Standard" into a gigantic money-making machine with at
least 85 percent of the country's oil business.

In 1889 a new figure appeared in Fairmont: the Standard Oil
tycoon and former U.S. Senator Johnson Newlon Camden, Sr.
He poured his money into construction of a thirty-three-mile
stretch of railroad between Fairmont and Clarksburg, used the

Watsons and Flemings as his agents to buy up 70,000 acres of prime coal land at prices ranging from $5 to $10 per acre, and launched an ambitious new mining concern, the Monogah Coal & Coke Company. At the same time James Edwin Watson, James Otis's son, joined him in starting the Montana Coal & Coke Company.

Camden was a robber baron in the worst sense of the term. He used his money to gain political power and then employed that power to make more money. With the Watson-Fleming-Haymond clique, and the opposing factions headed by Henry Davis and Stephen Elkins, he set the standards for political and economic morality in the state. He shares with those men the odium for having saddled West Virginia with a tragic legacy of political corruption and cynicism.

Camden was born near Jacksonville, Virginia (now West Virginia), in 1828 and grew up with his neighbor and friend Thomas "Stonewall" Jackson. Like Jackson, he attended the United States Military Academy, but not for long. He studied law and became prosecuting attorney in rural Nicholas County; he plowed his fees into tracts of cheap, undeveloped land and worked as a clerk for the Exchange Bank of Virginia. His salary, legal fees, and profits from land speculation went into immense new parcels of "vacant" land in central West Virginia. His legal clientele widened to include the Weston and Gauley Turnpike Company, the Exchange Bank, and a couple of Baltimore wholesale houses. He became a director of the Bank of Weston and ventured (unsuccessfully) into politics by running for the Virginia House of Delegates.[6]

Reflecting on the declining catch of whales and the resulting dearth of lighting fuel, Camden planned ventures to distill cannel coal into coal oil. James Otis Watson was already doing this in his "oil works" at Fairmont, but developments in Wirt County rendered such undertakings needless. In 1860 William Palmer Rathbone brought in a "flowing well" of petroleum at Burning Springs. He intended to sell it (as did John D. Rockefeller's father, William) as a sure-fire cure for cancer, but the well produced far more than the medicine market could absorb. In the rush to the new oil field, Johnson Newlon Camden led the pack. His uncle, Gideon Camden, owned much land in the vicinity, and the younger Camden quickly bought up tracts from the somnolent, isolated farmers.

Camden and Val Rathbone (whose grandson, Monroe Jackson Rathbone, became president of Standard Oil of New Jersey a century later) formed a partnership and started drilling. Before the end of the year their wells were producing 600 barrels daily. The energetic Camden forgot about his once-limited horizons as a bank director, clerk, prosecutor, and lawyer in Nicholas County, and he plunged into the brand-new world of oil. He built a refinery at Parkersburg and organized J. N. Camden & Company. The Camden-Rathbone enterprises grew apace, with more wells, storage tanks, pipelines, barges, and enlarged refineries. When John D. Rockefeller assembled the South Improvement Company, Camden was an eager collaborator. It evolved into the Standard Oil Company, into which J. N. Camden & Company was merged in 1875 and thereafter operated as Camden Consolidated Oil Company. Camden was issued 200 shares of Standard Oil stock at the inception of that petroleum colossus. (John D. Rockefeller held 3,000 shares.) He was a faithful and effective servitor of the trust and, like the Rockefellers and his other co-conspirators, observed with complete fidelity the trust-imposed vows of confidentiality.[7]

As the oil boom spread across West Virginia, Camden and Standard Oil were in the forefront. He lobbied at Charleston and other state capitals and in Washington for Standard's legislative goals; twice nominated for governor (1870 and 1872), he was defeated each time. However, judiciously placed Standard money (plus some of his own) finally convinced the legislature that Camden was a leader of unique wisdom and steadfastness, and he was elected to the U.S. Senate in 1881.

On the whole, Camden was eminently qualified to serve as a senator from Standard Oil. He used his influence to recruit co-investors in West Virginia railroads and in gigantic lumber operations. Their combined millions built the Weston & West Fork Railroad, the Clarksburg, Weston & Glenville Railroad & Transportation Company, the Weston & Buckhannon, and the Camden Interstate Railway. There followed lines from Wheeling to Parkersburg, from Parkersburg to Point Pleasant, and from

Huntington to Kenova. His mills cleared the virgin timber from 200,000 acres of central West Virginia land. Camden organized the Upper Monongahela Coal & Coke Company and was elected president of the Monongahela River Railroad Company. Eventually these regional railroads were merged into the systems of the Baltimore & Ohio, and thence into the Chesapeake & Ohio. The mergers resulted in stock issues to Camden and his heirs, and concomitant influence in the management of the parent companies. Through the vicissitudes of war and peace, the coal carriers of West Virginia and Kentucky have ground out dependable dividends for all who hold their shares.

Camden wanted to name his new coal town "Camden," but a post office with that name already existed. He settled for "Monogah," and the authorities named the post office "Jayenne," for his first and middle initials. The gleaming new rails of his Fairmont & Clarksburg line served thirty-three mines. Clearly a super-mogul had arrived in the coal capital of northern West Virginia.

In his *History of the Consolidation Coal Company* Charles Beachley, the secretary of the corporation, described one of the tactics used by the Fairmont ring to purchase coal cheaply from uncomprehending farmers:

> When Johnson N. Camden made his first trip over the Clarksburg-Fairmont territory, he carried a shot-gun with him to give the impression that he was on a squirrel hunt. He spent about two weeks alternately hunting and talking to the farmers in the region, and finally he arrived in Fairmont. While there he was the house guest of former Governor Fleming, and before leaving the Fleming homestead he presented the shot-gun to George Fleming—the governor's oldest son. . . . Following this first visit of Senator Camden, a great number of local farmers—under the belief that their coal would not be developed for "ages"—sold out for as low as the almost unbelievable price of $13.00 per acre.[8]

In 1893 the people of the state, acting through their legislators at Charleston, returned Camden to the senate. He distinguished himself by fighting ferociously for high tariffs on imported coal. He tenaciously defended Standard Oil against attacks by its "misguided" and "uninformed" detractors. He pointed out the folly of railroad rate regulation, helped form a

much maligned "sugar trust," and was charged with false
swearing. Camden's life was a sensational success story, but the
most sensational part of it came at 2:20 P.M. on December 5,
1907, at the huge Fairmont Coal Company mine at Monongah.
The mine (owned by Camden and members of the Watson family, with Clarence Wayland Watson serving as president) experienced a spectacular explosion which roared through the tunnels
and inundated the most distant working rooms with flames.
The concrete sidewalks of the town buckled; deep fissures
opened; buildings shook, and some collapsed. The official report listed 361 dead, but there were many more—a total of at
least 457. The grim official roster included 171 Italians, 85
Americans, 52 Hungarians, 31 Russians, 15 Austrians, and 5
Turks. The nationalities of the others were not listed by the
Congressional Select Committee to Investigate the Cause of
Mine Explosions.[9]

This ghastly event—the deadliest mine catastrophe in American history—might have been attributed to open-flame carbide
lamps, coal dust, inadequate ventilation, or outright ignorance
and unconcern on the part of management. Such attributions
were avoided, however, and the company and the United Mine
Workers of America agreed in putting the blame elsewhere—on
the low intelligence of Camden's imported miners. Said *Mines
and Minerals* in July, 1908, the problem of explosions "is due to
the large number of aliens. . . . These men are for the most part
illiterate, and of a lower standard of intelligence than their
predecessors of some years ago."[10]

Though there was no legal liability, the Fairmont Coal Company organized a relief committee which paid each of the 250
widows $150 plus $75 per orphan. When the Austrian ambassador complained about these minuscule payments to the sur-
vivors of Austrian immigrant miners, the company's attorney,
Aretas Brooks Fleming, replied in icy tones: "The company has
never contributed anything to persons here or abroad otherwise
than as a gratuity or donation. The company never for a mo-
ment considered that it was legally liable. . . . I think the $2,000
distributed principally among 41 children and 20 widows
would be quite a Christmas present." The relief committee

solicited all the money except the $2,000 given by the Fairmont Coal Company. The contributions came from all over the country, most of them from outside the coal fields.[11]

Fleming, a University of Virginia graduate, was an ambitious lawyer and politician. He was admitted to the bar in 1860 and opened a law office with his kinsman, Alpheus Haymond, who in 1872 was elected to the state's supreme court. Fleming was elected to the legislature in 1872 and 1874. He was an attorney for the Baltimore & Ohio and the Standard Oil Company before becoming a circuit judge in 1878. After ten years on the bench he was promoted by the Camden-Watson group as a candidate for governor, and he was elected in 1888. When his term expired he operated a coal mine and served as counsel for Camden and for numerous companies, including the Fairmont Coal Company and the Monongahela Railroad. He was a director of most of the companies he represented.

As governor and advocate, Fleming was a sword and buckler for his fellow moguls. He found labor unions pernicious, denounced anti-trust laws, vetoed increased appropriations for schools, sent the militia to break up strikes fomented by "outsiders," and praised the state's utterly permissive treatment of coal and rail corporations. He read the riot act to officials who objected to pouring acid mine drainage into the state's streams. Meanwhile he received a legal retainer fee of $10,000 annually from Standard Oil and held in his portfolio 11,000 shares in Fairmont Coal Company stock.[12]

Fleming served the Camden-Watson interests so loyally and effectively that in 1903 he was made chief counsel for, and a director of, the immensely expanded Consolidation Coal Company. His wife was a sister of Clarence Wayland Watson and a daughter of old James Otis. As a public official he served everyone except the people.[13]

In his official photograph as a U.S. Senator, J. N. Camden is the very essence of calm assurance. His is the equanimity of one whose well-earned millions are secure against attack, a commander of men and money. The state's official photograph of Governor Fleming is wholly different. A comparison of the two reveals master and servant as clearly as if one brandished a whip

and the other cowered in chains. Fleming appears as one who
has been summoned and instructed more times than are good
for dignity and peace of mind.

Clarence Wayland Watson, the youngest child of "the father
of the West Virginia coal industry," began his career in 1893. A
graduate of the Fairmont Normal School, he worked at his
father's operations, gaining experience and insights until he was
nearly thirty. He talked his brothers into joining him in a new
operation, the Briar Hill Coal Company. The company prospered as the nation recovered from the recession and panic of
1893, and the brothers organized or bought substantial new interests in other firms—the Gaston Coal Company, West Virginia Coal & Coke Company, and Montana Coal & Coke
Company. They did not forget their sisters but named two
towns, Ida May and Carolina, for them.

The audacious Clarence Watson perceived that cooperation
could bring greater profits than competition, and on June 20,
1901, he brought the Watson and Camden mines together into a
new entity, the Fairmont Coal Company (the firm whose mine
experienced the December 5, 1907, explosion already described).
Several other operators merged their companies into it also, for
a total of twenty mines and camps. A major part of the Upper
Monongahela industry now operated under a single management. The youthful industrialist had brought off his first great
coup.[14]

In 1902 the Watson brothers acquired their first property in
another state—the Somerset Coal Company in Pennsylvania. In
1903 they organized a syndicate and purchased the Baltimore &
Ohio's large interest in the Consolidation Coal Company; the
53,532 shares were transferred to Crawford Black, Jere Wheelwright, and Clarence Wayland Watson. By these rapid moves
the Watsons obtained immense leverage in the nation's coal industry, but their acquisitions were by no means completed.
They conferred with other operators in Maryland, Pennsylvania, and the upper Monongahela in West Virginia. Through a
combination of persuasion and intimidation that anticipated
the great merger era of the 1960's, they brought into Consolidation Coal most of the operators in the three huge fields.[15]

In May, 1909, Watson caught the eye of the nation by uniting the Fairmont and the huge Somerset properties into Consolidation Coal, thereby creating an industrial behemoth. The Somerset Coal Company alone owned 20,000 acres and produced nearly 2 million tons of coal annually—a tremendous capacity at the time.

The post-merger Consolidation Coal was reorganized with $20 million of new capital. On May 14, 1909, the *New York Times* reported that John D. Rockefeller was the chief supporter of "the great soft coal combination" that included all the erstwhile properties of Consolidation Coal Company, Fairmont Coal Company, the Somerset Company, the Pittsburgh & Fairmont Fuel Company, and the Clarksburg Fuel Company. According to the *Times*, the combination controlled 200,000 acres and would deal in a large variety of coals, with offices and agencies in New York, Baltimore, Philadelphia, Cincinnati, Detroit, and Chicago.

The Maryland Mining Company of 1828 had grown into a colossus. A young entrepreneur had brought together under one shield and banner the best part of the American coal industry, eliminating bruising competition and allying old and new moguls. As matters stood, "Consol" could mine 10 million tons annually. The enlarged Consolidated Coal assembled by Watson was largely a creation of West Virginians. The original Maryland company was capitalized at $10,250,000, the Somerset at $4,000,000, and the Fairmont at $17,500,000. At the time of the merger Fairmont alone possessed 37 fully equipped mines, 1,060 coke ovens, annual production of 3.8 million tons, and the capacity to increase output by an additional 5 million tons.

The management did not plan to stand still, however. With Rockefeller to fund them, huge new expansions were inevitable. President Charles K. Lord resigned, and Clarence Wayland Watson replaced him. Jere Wheelwright, Senator Camden's secretary, represented the senator on the board and served as vice-president while Crawford Black sat as spokesman for the old east coast investors. The real control over the combine was in the hands of President Watson, Johnson Newlon Camden, Sr., and his son J. N. Camden, Jr., James Otis Watson II, James Edwin Watson, Sylvanus Lamb Watson, A. Brooks Fleming and his son George, a couple of their cousins, progeny of old Judge

Alpheus Haymond, and Van Lear Black, the energetic and rising son of Crawford Black.

The older capitalists in New York, Baltimore, and Massachusetts may have been somewhat unsettled, and perhaps even a little frightened, by these fast-moving and far-reaching events. In any event, the surviving founders of the George's Creek mining field, and the heirs of those who had passed on to the eternal coal boom in the sky, were ready to participate fully in a Kentucky bonanza.

FIVE

The Strange Rise of John C. C. Mayo

THE RUGGED TERRAIN of eastern Kentucky guaranteed that most of its inhabitants would be poor. Except in the lower reaches of the main rivers, the valleys were narrow. The soil was composed of weathered sandstone and shale mixed with immense accumulations of decayed vegetation and laid down on clay. When the land was first plowed it produced fabulous crops, but rains lifted the soft, fertile loam and floated it away, leaving behind depleted earth which repeated planting and harvesting reduced to near sterility. As the bottomlands lost their fruitfulness, "new grounds" were cleared on the hillsides and the land ruin increased. Silt from the eroding hillsides filled the water holes, and the schools of black bass declined. The people loved to hunt, and by the 1880's deer and other large game had vanished. Despite massive emigration to new land in southern Ohio and Indiana, Arkansas, Oklahoma, Missouri, Texas, Oregon, and Washington, population pressures mounted. Worries over tenuous land titles weighed on the minds of people in the region. Thirty years after the Civil War, mountaineers were subsisting largely on sales of trees from the retreating forests.[1]

Thousands of families still lived in log houses much like those built a century earlier by Boone and Kenton. The meal sack was the chief source of food; the diet consisted largely of cornbread, fried hog meat, coffee, sorghum molasses, eggs, and (when the cow was not dry) milk and butter.

Along hundreds of tributary streams the people had cut their clearings to the upper reaches of the hollows and nearly to the weathered rimrock. Although huge areas remained uncleared, these represented only a remnant of the once magnificent deciduous forest. Something had to be done if the people were to survive. In that era before the rise of the welfare state, governments were powerless. Food could be gotten onto most tables only by the actions of private citizens—businessmen from beyond the hills, and a tiny handful of native highlanders.[2]

The "hillbilly" has been portrayed as a shuffling, stooped, lanky moonshiner and, in recent decades, as a shy, inarticulate coal miner afflicted by unemployment and pneumoconiosis. The former existed in abundance in earlier times, and unassailable data reveal the latter in huge numbers throughout the mine fields today.

But always there have been highlanders of another breed, a self-assured, dynamic minority for whom the "outside world" has held no terrors. They have faced that world, lived with it, and dominated it. Two of the greatest heroes of World War I were of this type—Alvin York of Fentress County, Tennessee, and Willie Sandlin of Breathitt County, Kentucky. Their exploits in the infantry battles of 1918 astounded the world.[3] Fred Vinson of Louisa, Kentucky, became a principal architect of America's industrial war effort in World War II, then secretary of the treasury, and chief justice of the United States. Little Knox County has generated nearly a dozen major political figures, including six congressmen, a U.S. Supreme Court justice, two governors of Kentucky, and a governor of Missouri.[4] In the 1970's migrants from the Kentucky hills included a senator from Iowa; Karl Bays, president of the American Hospital Supply Corporation; Orell Collins, president and chief executive officer of Nalco Chemical Corporation; a chemistry group leader in the radioactive isotopes section of Oak Ridge National Laboratories; a senior engineer at Fisher Body Division of General Motors; and several of the wealthiest businessmen in Kentucky. In President Jimmy Carter's cabinet Juanita Morris Kreps, who grew up in a tiny coal camp called Clutts in Harlan County, served as secretary of commerce.

This phenomenon of excellence and achievement rising out of a generally poor and uneducated population is of long standing.

The Lincoln family that gave the nation the Great Emancipator moved west from the rocky hills of Virginia's upper valley. Occasionally circumstances allow a mountaineer to surmount all adversities—isolation, poor schools, lack of books, poverty, and, in recent times, too much television—and to become a spectacular success in science, politics, or business.

Perhaps the most startling of these success stories lies in the strange career of John Caldwell Calhoun Mayo, who was born on September 16, 1864, on an exhausted mountain farm in Pike County. In those days rural hill people drew almost their entire subsistence from the soil—corn, vegetables, milk, "sweetening," meat, and the flax and wool that composed the rough linsey-woolsey that covered their backs. The Mayo family lived in this hard and simple fashion when their son was born near the end of the Civil War. In those days diapers were unknown, at least in the Kentucky hills, and toddlers were clothed in a weaning dress ("wamus") shaped like an old-fashioned nightgown. In the families of the very poor this humble garment was made longer as the child grew taller, and it was not uncommon to see a gawky teenager draped in such raiment and no other. This custom, rooted in antiquity, was frequently seen among the rural people of England and Scotland when the ancestors of the southern highlanders began "making the crossing" in the 1600's.

In 1879, when John C. C. Mayo was fifteen, his father sent him to the home of a sick neighbor to cut some wood for the voracious fireplace. Barefoot and clad in one of those simple garments,[5] the boy chopped the wood into suitable pieces. The ailing neighbor's five-year-old son watched the woodchopper at work. He and Mayo liked each other from that first meeting. They rose in the world together—Mayo to become Kentucky's wealthiest man, and John Buckingham, as his student and business associate, to become his banker and a co-executor of his will.

While untold thousands of Appalachian youths have grown up illiterate, Mayo was different. His father moved to a somewhat more promising farm down the Big Sandy in Johnson County, and the boy got up on frosty mornings and made his way to the log schoolhouse. The heat came from a cavernous fireplace, the floor was made of puncheons, and the seats were split-log benches. Like Abraham Lincoln, Mayo began life with an axe in his hand and learned his letters in a boisterous blab school presided over by a teacher who had never seen a college. If environment were the chief determinant of human destiny, it is unlikely that either man would have escaped the drudgery of axe, maul, glut, and plow.[6]

Mayo, a voracious learner, read all the books that were available in the Johnson County backwoods. Since the requirements for a "common school" teacher in Kentucky in the 1880's were just about any that a semi-literate trustee might specify, at sixteen he became qualified to teach. He already recognized his immense need for more learning, and his resolution to obtain a decent education must have startled people throughout the countryside.

In due time, Mayo did something almost unheard of in the hills in that era: wearing better raiment bought with borrowed money and riding on a mule, he made his way to the nearest railhead and caught a train to Kentucky Wesleyan College at Millersburg. Money was so scarce that Thomas Jefferson Mayo had had to mortgage his hard-won farm to raise money for his son's venture into higher education.

The student lived with extreme frugality and worked much of the time to raise additional funds. His skill in mathematics led to a job as a part-time instructor for less gifted students. When he graduated in 1886, he had a bachelor's degree and a first-class certificate as a teacher in the public schools. A photograph of Mayo as a senior at Kentucky Wesleyan shows his face resolute and intelligent. He is neatly, almost primly dressed in a dark suit, bow tie, and ruffled white shirt. His wavy hair is properly trimmed and his eyes are calm, direct, and self-assured. Here is no member of a lost generation, no rootless wanderer trying to "find himself."

Mayo had not limited his college studies to spelling, composition, history, grammar, and arithmetic. He heard lectures in geology by Professor A. C. Sherwood and learned for the first time about the extensive mineral resources of his native hills. The college library contained copies of the voluminous geological surveys made at state expense by Mather, Owen, Shaler, and Proctor, and he spent hours poring over them and filling notebooks with data and comments. When he returned home, schemes and visions were forming in his head.

Hill society had been so sundered by the Civil War that the schools in Johnson County were segregated not by race, but by politics. For several years Mayo taught in the "Democratic school" at Paintsville for $40 per month—a considerable sum in those days. Mayo saved enough to pay off the troublesome mortgage on his parents' farm. Because Paintsville had no bank, he then accumulated, a few dollars at a time, $150 in cash. With that modest capital Mayo set out to transform the Kentucky hills and their people.

In 1892 he found partners, John W. Castle and Dr. I. R. Turner, who were willing to risk a few of their hard-earned dollars, and the trio formed the trading firm of Castle, Turner & Mayo, Inc. Each partner contributed $150, and with the total of $450 Mayo began building his empire. His methods were simple. He combed through the deed books in county court houses, identified the landowners with the best semblance of titles, and compared their holdings against his notes made in the Kentucky Wesleyan College library. Where titles to valuable minerals appeared worth the risk, he approached a landowner (whom Mayo generally viewed as a mere squatter) and offered him fifty cents or a dollar for an option to buy the minerals underlying his land. The option or "agreement to purchase" was for a term of several years and provided for ultimate payments of from fifty cents to five or six dollars per acre. Almost all farmers were eager to execute the options. They signed their names (or, in most instances, affixed their marks) and prayed that Mayo could raise the purchase money within the time specified.

The budding entrepreneur faced a difficult task, but not a hopeless one. With $450 he could secure options to buy the minerals under a lot of farms. Eventually Mayo bought out his partners, retained the options in his own name, and continued buying with small sums saved from his teaching salary.[7] Remembering the parents who had mortgaged their home to educate him, he repaid them with the gift of a much more fertile farm north of Paintsville.

In 1890, at the age of twenty-six, Mayo had engineered a tremendously important change in the state's basic law. (By this time he had read law and become a lawyer.) When a convention assembled at Frankfort to write a new constitution, Mayo was not among the delegates, but his friend and kinsman A. J. Auxier was. Auxier was an adroit lawyer and an able and aggressive debater; he and Mayo had often discussed those ancient Virginia grants that encumbered the land titles and the very future of Kentucky. The state's previous constitutions had contained an express sanction of the "Virginia Compact" that rendered those grants inviolable. At Mayo's urging, Auxier skillfully argued for the omission of that sanction in the new document, on the grounds that it reduced Kentucky to a client or vassal of Virginia. Auxier was supported in his efforts by F. A. Hopkins, a fellow mountaineer from Letcher, Knott, and Floyd Counties, and by W. M. Beckner of Clark County. The convention accepted Auxier's reasoning, and the compact was omitted when the people approved the state's charter in 1892. Mayo had begun a process that would forever nullify most of those burdensome and hoary patents.[8]

Mayo handled all his undertakings with microscopic attention to detail. For generations people recounted his skills as a teacher. His humble classroom was kept meticulously clean; the blackboard was regularly washed and adorned with poetry, which he required his students to memorize and repeat on demand. He loaded them down with homework and insisted that they do it. He brought fresh flowers to brighten the drab place, and he managed to inspire many of his charges with a vision of the vast world beckoning beyond the hilltops.[9]

In 1893 he contacted the Merritt brothers—Leonidas, Napoleon, Louis, Cassius, and Alfred—of Duluth, Minnesota, who were known in the world of steel as "the Iron Brothers." These self-made tycoons began life as farmboys at Chautauqua, New York, entered the iron business, and explored the region west of Lake Superior in search of ore fields. They marked out the best part of the Mesabi iron range and bought it cheaply, before the unsuspecting backwoodsmen realized the significance of what lay beneath the harsh, pine-grown hills. Mayo persuaded the brothers that a gigantic steel industry could be built in the area of Ironton, Ohio, and Ashland, Kentucky—a region where, in Mayo's words, "coal and iron meet." They undertook to buy the Detroit, Michigan & Ironton Railroad and to bring the ore to Ironton or Ashland for smelting. To the complete astonishment of everyone in Johnson County, Mayo sold the Merritts 29,000 acres of mineral rights for $100,000 in cash and an interest-bearing promissory note for an additional $100,000. He came home, consummated the transactions with the delighted farmers, and transferred his title to the Merritts. Suddenly, "Little John Mayo" was the talk of the mountains.[10]

Unfortunately, the Merritts had mortgaged the iron range to John D. Rockefeller for $500,000, and they defaulted in the panic that hit the country later that year. Rockefeller (whom the Mellons of Pittsburgh referred to as "Pendragon" and Andrew Carnegie called "Wreckafellow") foreclosed and became the owner of North America's richest iron ore deposit. When the Merritts were unable to pay Mayo's note, he, who had borrowed heavily against it and plowed all his money back into more options and land purchases, faced ruin.[11] He had acquired options on an additional 100,000 acres of superb coking coal but was without funds to pay off the farmers and take the deeds.

Mayo turned to the courts and quickly attached those 29,000 acres he had sold to the Merritts. When his claim was upheld he retrieved the land, thereby beginning a financial recovery. W. S. Dudley and three of his neighbors at Carlisle, Kentucky, came to his rescue with a loan of $20,000 secured by his company's bond. These funds were promptly used to buy up land under the maturing options and Mayo became "land poor"—he owned tens of thousands of acres of valuable minerals, but he possessed no money. He returned to his friend John Buckingham and borrowed a few dollars for printing and postage; then he prepared flyers describing his mineral lands and mailed them to dozens of industrialists in Baltimore, New York, Boston, Washington, Cincinnati, and elsewhere.

One of the form letters fell into the receptive hands of Peter L. Kimberly, a Pennsylvanian and president of the Sharon Steel & Hoop Company. Kimberly sent Mayo a telegram inviting him to come to Chicago for a conference. Calhoun (as he was sometimes called) went back to the faithful Buckingham, who found fifty dollars to finance the trip.[12]

The wire from Kimberly had come in the nick of time. Options on thousands of acres had expired or were about to, and imploring mountaineers were hot on Mayo's tracks. They begged him to purchase their minerals and threatened otherwise to sell them to bidders who were drifting in from Virginia, New York, and Boston. Mayo urged them to be patient and promised them more than any of these latecomers would pay. In this he kept his word: though he paid little for his fabulous acquisitions, he routinely paid more than his competitors in the land market.

Mayo returned from Chicago a different man. He wore a new suit and, with it, an air of confidence. He had signed a contract under which Kimberly's company would pay him five dollars per acre for mineral lands in Letcher, Pike, and Floyd Counties. Mayo retained a 25 percent interest in all such lands—including, of course, participation in such royalties as they might produce when mining began. He had a check for $10,000 and authority to draw on Kimberly's account for additional funds as needed for his operations. The woodchopper-schoolteacher-lawyer was about to become a full-fledged mogul, his rags turned to riches, his empty pockets bulging with money.

Mayo understood the crass, materialistic natures of his fellow citizens and set out at once to bend them to his will. He brought in a new rolltop desk and other impressive office furniture, the first items of their kind ever seen in the Big Sandy backwoods. He opened the huge cartons on the street so that passersby could gawk at the splendid items while his rented offices were being refurbished. He took Kimberly's check for $10,000—an enormous sum for that penurious place—and showed it to all and sundry. He brought in large bundles of cash, including bags of shiny gold coins, and flashed them before the eyes of his visitors. When his office had been painted and furnished, he conducted scores of people through it so they could feast their eyes on his desk, conference tables, upholstered chairs, rugs, typewriters, and shelves of new law books. He told his dumbfounded guests about his contract with Kimberly's Sharon Steel & Hoop Company and the magnitude of the company's operations. This flamboyance and bravado paid off. The word spread like wildfire through a dozen counties: Mayo is the man with the money! Sell to him and avoid other would-be purchasers! He is the man of the future![13]

Mayo rarely bought land outright; he preferred to buy the underlying "coal, oil, gas, salt and salt water, stone, shale, and other mineral and metallic substances," together with the right to mine and remove them by all means "deemed necessary or convenient." This left the seller (the farmer) in possession of the surface and the right to use it for "agricultural purposes not inconsistent with" the rights of the mineral owners. In other words, in any contest between the two, the rights of the miners were dominant. The farmer would pay the greater part of the taxes, since his estate was clearly visible and measurable while the mineral estate lay hidden underground—undetermined, perhaps nonexistent.[14]

Mayo paid off Buckingham, bought himself a fine horse and an impressive buckboard, laid in a supply of good cigars and mellow whiskey, stocked up on printed blank option and deed forms, and, with crisp new paper currency and freshly minted gold coins to impress the yokels, headed into the hinterland of eroded farms, atrocious creek-bottom roads, stands of towering oak and tulip trees, destitution, ignorance, and greed. Sometimes he was rebuffed by an adamant landowner, but more often when he returned dusty and trail-worn to his office he had stacks of options and deeds for recording. He operated in Johnson, Floyd, Pike, Perry, Leslie, and Letcher Counties, and people vied with one another to keep him in their homes overnight and to sign his documents. His generosity was legendary because after the conclusion of a successful trade he generally handed the worn, weary wife a five-dollar gold piece as an "outright gift." Often the only money the woman had ever possessed, the coins were sometimes preserved for half a century and shown proudly to heirs and visitors as "my John Mayo money."

Legends grew up around his success story, turning him into a towering folk hero. Mountaineers thought he would make a great governor. Mayo murmured deprecatingly that he desired only to "develop the hills," and to provide jobs and economic opportunities.

Though Mayo was intensely devoted to his business dealings, by the time he entered his thirties he began to consider marriage. His bride, Alice Meeks, was sixteen, just half her groom's age at the time of their wedding in 1897. The lissome young woman was one of his students, and she had impressed him as precisely the kind of wife an ambitious man required. He judged well, for she was his sturdy right arm throughout the remaining seventeen years of his life. (The new Mrs. Mayo's support of her husband purportedly began on a financial basis, soon after the wedding; he was at that time so "land poor" that he took her to a visiting circus on fifty cents that *she* had borrowed from John Buckingham!)

Sometimes Alice Mayo accompanied her husband on his land-buying forays. She put stacks of twenty-dollar gold pieces into long, narrow leather bags which she carried under her voluminous skirts. When she brought out those glittering coins, men reeled in fits of avarice. Women thought she was the "purtiest" lady they had ever seen. John and Alice became favored children's names along lonesome, forlorn valleys where drudgery, boredom, and futility had reigned unchallenged for a hundred years.[15]

As the new century arrived, Mayo was a wealthy man by Kentucky standards, although his net worth (approximately $250,000) was by no means enough to mark him as a mogul. His successes up to that point simply goaded him to look for ways of swelling his fortune quickly.

John C. C. Mayo, 1912. (Mayo Companies, Ashland, Ky.)

Mayo family: John C. C. Mayo and wife, left rear; Washington Irving Mayo and wife, right rear; Thomas Jefferson Mayo and wife, foreground, with John's children flanking their grandfather. (Mayo Companies.)

Mayo mansion, Paintsville, Ky., today. (Anne F. Caudill.)

Financiers inspecting coal vein in Letcher County, 1911. John C. C. Mayo is third from right. The man on horseback is Clarence Wayland Watson; also in the group are Jere Wheelwright and Johnson N. Camden, Jr. (Courtesy of Charles Stallard, Jenkins, Ky.)

Funeral of John C. C. Mayo. His mansion is at the center; Mayo Memorial Methodist Church is on the right. (Mayo Companies.)

Moguls at Fleming, Ky., the day after attending John C. C. Mayo's funeral. Three mounted men at center are George Fleming, Thomas Haymond, and Clarence Wayland Watson; third from left is Campbell Bascom Slemp, congressman from Big Stone Gap, Va. (Courtesy of Ivan Kimbrell, Haymond, Ky.)

SIX

The Ring Closes In

SOON AFTER 1900 a group of moguls, primarily those from the Fairmont ring, introduced the new and ruthless breed of politics that has now ruled Kentucky for nearly three generations. Though the architects of the new order have long since gone to the cemeteries and the political dynasty that they created has weakened somewhat in the hands of their successors, the rule of coal still prevails on most issues. The "filthy hand" is still at the throat of Kentucky sixty years after Alben Barkley vowed to break its hold.

The moguls perfected a new politics—the politics of money —which some West Virginia journalists vociferously denounced as "Watsonism."[1] Before the advent of Watsonism, Kentucky was run by windy and generally rather witless orators who drank too much bourbon and had only the scantiest notions of public policy. They did not mind the trifling salaries allowed by the Commonwealth's series of curious, old-fashioned constitutions; they wore chin whiskers and string ties, reveled in overblown military titles, and occasionally achieved some small progress during their "administrations."[2]

With the advent of Watsonism things changed. The new politicians were not vapid, small-town lawyers with scanty ambitions; they were highly successful, hard-driving, tough businessmen and fortune builders who knew what they wanted and how to get and keep it. What they wanted was money, and the power and prestige of public office with which to fend off "undue" tax burdens and troublesome laws. Fortune was of far greater importance to them than fame.

John C. C. Mayo helped bring to the attention of the Fairmont ring the vast riches of eastern Kentucky. As he sought ways to increase industrial development in the area, and hence to further his own financial interests, it was inevitable that he should turn to Baltimore, headquarters of the old coal tycoons of the western Maryland field, and to Fairmont, West Virginia, where Johnson Newlon Camden and the sons of James Otis Watson were forging new coal empires. With supreme brashness and silver-tongued eloquence Mayo began making the rounds of their offices. What these field marshals of high finance thought about him in those first encounters is unknown, but that they came to hold him in great affection and respect cannot be doubted.

To the Camdens, the Watson brothers, Aretas Brooks Fleming and his sons A. B. and George, and Thomas N. Haymond, Mayo explained the facts about eastern Kentucky's mineral wealth.[3] It lay there—coal, oil, gas, and chemical brines in vast and documented beds. In a letter to George C. Jenkins dated October 25, 1909, Jere Wheelwright described the quality of the gigantic mineral treasure Mayo had pinned down: "The coals of Eastern Kentucky are of a character which are essential in the arts of metallurgy, in processes where modern practice demands pure products. . . . The coals of the Northern Coal and Coke Company property belong to the highest coking class. This places it at once in the manufacture of pig-iron, in copper, smelters and numerous other industries of less magnitude where coke is essential in the manufacture."[4]

The local people had, in the main, dubious titles which they were eager to sell for less than a third of the going prices for similar properties in West Virginia, and Mayo knew how to protect those titles against all claimants once they were purchased and the deeds recorded. In their richly furnished mansions and in their offices above the bustling lobbies of their banks, the moguls listened to him, and were persuaded. In 1902 Peter Kimberly joined the Fairmont ring in forming a new company under the laws of West Virginia. Capitalized at $500,000 and with power to recapitalize at will, it could buy, hold, and sell minerals and mineral lands and it could mine and drill for them. Johnson Newlon Camden, Sr., was elected president of the Northern Coal & Coke Company.

Mayo and his wife went to work forthwith to augment the already immense holdings represented by stacks of options and deeds. The birth of two children (a son and a daughter) soon knocked Alice out of the buying campaign, but Mayo continued alone. He traveled hundreds of miles on mules, horses, or buckboards as the quality of the trails dictated, sleeping on shuck and feather beds in stifling cabins and eating with apparent zest the notoriously poor cookery of mountain hearths. His persistence and persuasiveness were rewarded with ever-growing collections of options which lawyers for Northern Coal & Coke labored in grimy courthouses to abstract and certify. By 1902 he had become eastern Kentucky's first millionaire.[5]

Mayo's ability to cozen the unlettered hill people rarely encountered failure. On one occasion he ran into formidable resistance in the person of Booker Mullins at the headwaters of Elk Horn Creek in Letcher County. The notoriously violent Mullins had sworn to shoot any man who tried to "beat him out of" his minerals. Mayo, who knew from Northern's engineers that the property would have to be acquired as part of the site of a proposed mining town, rode to Mullins's house and found his quarry glaring at him from a rocking chair on the front porch. Mayo introduced himself and immediately produced a roll of two hundred new five-dollar bills. He told Mullins they would be his if he would agree to hear him for a mere ten minutes. The offer proved irresistible, and at the end of their conversation Mullins sold. He used the $10,000 to buy a Bluegrass farm, but he was so dissatisfied in the "lowlands" that he later returned to the hills, passionately hating Mayo for having talked him out of his beloved land. The town of Jenkins now sprawls across his lost and lamented acres.[6]

In 1907 Mayo negotiated a stupendous deal with the officers of Consolidation Coal. Around the conference table sat some of the most able businessmen in America; they included Consolidation's President Clarence Wayland Watson, A. B. Fleming, A. T. Watson, George W. Fleming, Frank Haas, Jonathan Jenkins, and John Gordon Smyth. Such an impressive battery of tycoons would have over-awed most country lawyers, but Mayo emerged rich and triumphant. In return for 20,000 acres he had a check for $50,000 plus enough Consol stock to give him a respectable voice in the company's management. The check, by far the largest ever seen in the Big Sandy Valley, set off new tremors of admiration and envy. The number of mountain boys named John Calhoun Mayo multiplied mightily.[7]

But Mayo came out of the Miller's Creek negotiations with something infinitely more valuable than the check and stock certificate. Coal lands were worthless without railroads to haul the fuel to mills and factories. Kentucky's ineffectual politicians and underfinanced business interest had struggled for decades to lure railroads into the heart of the state's hill country, but their accomplishments had been meager and slow. Consol, with its roots at Baltimore and Fairmont and in the Rockefeller colossus, assured that lines would be built from the terminus at Stafford, Kentucky, to the company's new holdings. Camden and his associates financed the Miller's Creek Railroad, a four-mile stretch from Consol's new holdings to the Chesapeake and Ohio. The tycoons moved so expeditiously that the first carload of coal left the Miller's Creek mine in 1910.

Richard Broas, the onetime Union Army captain who had pioneered the surveying and acquisition of the Elk Horn coal field, had haunted the Big Sandy and Kentucky headwaters for a quarter-century without being able to develop his 11,000 acres. Discouraged, sick, and no longer young, he sold his land to Mayo for Northern Coal & Coke. On November 28, 1910, the Broas tract and much more—a gigantic sprawl of 104,000 acres—was sold by Northern Coal & Coke to Consolidation. By January 2, 1911, when other deeds from Northern vested additional lands in Consol, the Mayo, Camden-Watson, Fleming-Haymond ring had control of what their engineers and chemists believed to contain a billion tons of the finest coal in North America. When Northern Coal & Coke was organized, Mayo had been granted a quarter of the stock, so the conveyance to Consol made him even wealthier. Part of his profits from that transaction were set aside to draw interest; the rest were invested in mineral options in eastern Pike County and along the Kentucky River in Letcher, Knott, Perry, and Breathitt. While the hill people lined up outside his office to sell some of the world's most important fuel beds, the railroads commenced building the extensions that would increase the value of those minerals a hundred times over.[8]

In 1902 the creaky Louisville & Nashville Railroad fell into the clutches of a man who knew how to raise money and spend it on huge projects. John Pierpont Morgan made the L&N a subsidiary of the Atlantic Coast Line. The board was shaken up a bit during the Morgan years, and the younger Warren Delano became a director. Mayo appealed to the L&N to build a track leading to the superb metallurgical and coking coals in Letcher County east of Whitesburg. Plagued by fear that competing lines might penetrate the region by cutting through the divide between the Kentucky and Big Sandy valleys, the L&N bought all the stock of the Lexington & Eastern, a short line that had been stuck for years at Jackson in Breathitt County. The L&N employed all the lawyers in Letcher County, including the county attorney and county judge, to investigate and buy right-of-way titles. Working under terrific pressure, contractors and their sweating crews of Italian stonemasons and black steel drivers and tracklayers pushed the single track line 101 miles to the extreme upper reaches of Boone Creek. The rails crossed the Kentucky on sixteen bridges and bored through a half-dozen new tunnels. The line was completed on November 23, 1912, rendering Mayo's stupendous holdings on the North Fork of the Kentucky no longer isolated and inaccessible. The new rails and the white oak ties beneath them bound his products to the markets of the world.

Clarence Wayland Watson was unwilling to wait for the B&O and the C&O to build lines into the heart of the vast Elk Horn field at the Pike-Letcher line. Under his prodding Consol's directors authorized the construction of a thirty-three-mile line, the Sandy Valley & Elk Horn, to the projected town of Jenkins—a narrow valley until lately the haunt of Booker Mullins and his neighbor, "Bad John" Wright. So relentlessly did Watson press the work that the final spike was driven in the early fall of 1912. The Rockefeller-controlled B&O promptly bought the new line; thus the tracks of the L&N and B&O terminated on opposite sides of a narrow ridge no more than a half-mile apart. In 1923 the Chesapeake & Ohio acquired the old Sandy Valley and Elk Horn trackage. The C&O's line had previously reached Hellier and Elkhorn City at the Breaks of the Sandy in 1902.

Mayo and his friends had shattered the isolation of the hills and bound the people to a new and radically different way of life. A disbelieving mountain woman watched the first train she had ever seen hissing and snorting its way to a new coal tipple on Potter's Fork. Immense clouds of black smoke belched from its stacks, and cinders and blobs of soot fell on all sides. The tracks rumbled with the weight of the ponderous engine and its line of groaning cars. "That thing had a hard time a'gittin' in here and it will never in this world git out," she predicted.[9]

A tradition that is deeply embedded in mountain lore has it that Mayo took an initiative that settled for all time the rights of the competing railroads in his immense new coal field. He wanted the cooperation of all railmen in devising a lasting and dependable transportation system that would serve all parts of the field, so he arranged for them a tour—or, rather, a strenuous overland journey—across the steep ridges and twisting valleys. The eastern bankers and financiers present included the presidents of the Baltimore & Ohio, the Western Maryland, and the Chesapeake & Ohio, plus a representative of the Louisville & Nashville. (The C&O had opposed the opening of the field on the ground that it would glut the markets.) He hired Oscar Tschirky, the world-famous principal chef at the Waldorf-Astoria Hotel, to accompany the travelers and provide food for them. Wine, champagne, caviar, and numerous other gourmet stores were shipped by rail and wagon to anticipated campsites. Oscar,[10] who reputedly could bow all the way to the floor without withdrawing his outstretched hand, prepared a superb repast which was served under a sycamore tree on Elk Horn Creek. There in the shade, well filled with good food and drink, the moguls apportioned the hills among their respective lines.

The story maintains that John D. Rockefeller made the trip and enjoyed it immensely; he laid down the law to the assembled tycoons and, quite predictably, the others agreed to his dictates. Buckingham relates that such a trip and meeting did in fact take place, but he makes no mention of Rockefeller's presence, and no other evidence of Pendragon's participation has been discovered. However, the late Harry LaViers, Sr., son of the founder of South-East Coal Company, stated shortly before his death that Rockefeller was there: "I know it to be a fact!"[11]

Oscar's "vittles" fascinated the native sons and their wives, who hovered about his camp to watch in silence as he sifted, kneaded, rolled, and baked. They watched chilled sparkling wine splash into delicate stemmed glasses, and they saw tender cutlets breaded and fried. They observed as men ate lettuce and celery salads and dainty servings of smoked oysters. Their almost universal opinion was that such grub would not be fit to eat.

It is possible that Rockefeller and a group of moguls came to eastern Kentucky in 1911, though the press's failure to report on such a visit seems inexplicable. The tradition, however, is so deeply rooted as to inspire respect. LaViers declared unequivocally that John Jacob Astor IV was one of the travelers and that he drowned on the *Titanic* the following year. Ivan "Red" Kimbrell, who was Clarence Watson's chauffeur for a time in the 1930's, has quoted "the senator" as saying that Mayo organized the tour and that the aggregate wealth of the travelers exceeded the assets of the United States Treasury at that time.[12]

Mayo's success now ballooned as he brought off a series of spectacular coups. In 1913, at his urging, the Fairmont ring organized the Elk Horn Fuel Company, soon to be renamed the Elk Horn Coal Corporation. To this new West Virginia corporation the Northern Coal & Coke Company conveyed most of the remainder of Mayo's huge acquisitions in the Elk Horn mineral field—the superlative deposits of coal, oil, and gas under 265,000 acres, the equivalent of a Kentucky county. This transfer made him a substantial stockholder in the new entity. He remained the owner in his individual name and right of approximately 20,000 acres in Johnson and Pike Counties, and he retained a controlling interest in 10,000 acres owned by the Tom's Creek Coal Company. His holdings in other corporations—Montrose Coal Company and Hamilton Realty—were merged into Elk Horn.[13]

With railroads converging from all sides, a juggernaut suddenly struck the primitive eastern Kentucky counties. These roadless rural slums with their dirty, foul-smelling courthouses took on a new image almost overnight. The region became an El Dorado (perhaps a "coaldorado" would be more apt) and men bore down upon it from around the globe. They trooped in from the exhausted valley of the Tennessee River, from the farmed-out cotton country of the Deep South, from the cities of the east coast, and from the older coal fields of Maryland and Pennsylvania. They were joined by multitudes from the immigrant ships—Italians, Croats, Serbs, Russians, Syrians, and even a few Swedes, Swiss, Albanians, and Jews. Whole valleys were drained of young men as the Kentucky hill people turned from subsistence farming to new lives as coal miners. In the sequestered valleys they built King Coal's new empire.[14]

Work on the new towns began long before the rails could reach the sites. Nicola Construction Company was the largest contractor, and the builders worked at an almost frenzied pace. Crude barracks were nailed together and tent towns were laid out, with cook houses, wells, and the inevitable rows of privies. Every available mule, horse, and ox was rounded up and set to hauling supplies over abominable roads which gangs of men with picks and shovels toiled to keep passable. Architects and supervising engineers staked out long rows where houses were to rise. Sawmills were dragged in on huge, specially built wagons. The whirring blades sliced boards from virgin timber, which were promptly dried in improvised kilns. Italians quarried on sandstone cliffs, and brickmakers dug clay and baked it. The limestone on the north face of the Pine Mountain was blasted out and transformed into lime and cement.

Consolidation built more than a thousand houses and other structures at its showplace on upper Elk Horn. "Management Row" (called by miners "Silk Stocking Row") rose above a glistening new lake, the town's source of water. (The lake was impounded by a concrete dam poured by a hundred dusty sons of Italy.) These spacious houses, set amid trees preserved from the original forest, provided the most pleasant residential area the hills have known.

Masons raised a power plant and a tall brick smokestack. Forty-four oxen dragged the steam boiler across the Pine Mountain from another new town in Wise County, Virginia— Norton, named for Eckstein Norton, president of the L&N. Workers laid down concrete streets and sidewalks and raised a hospital, a hotel, office buildings, a movie theater and recreation building, machine shops, stores or commissaries, and churches and schools. The place was named for George C. Jenkins, a

Baltimore banker who was pouring money into it. Jenkins was a director of the Atlantic Coal Line, the Louisville & Nashville, and the Baltimore & Ohio. He sat on the boards of the Merchants-Mechanics National Bank, Maryland Trust Company, Maryland Life Insurance Company, and, of course, Consolidation Coal. A good Catholic who never permitted his Christian scruples to stymie his profits, he built a small church on a hillside and gave it to the diocese. St. George was chosen as the congregation's patron saint—"In honor," as one scribe put it, "of George C. Jenkins."[15]

Smoky Row, Mud Town, Wright's Hollow, Camden, Dunham, Burdine, Lakeside—the sections of the new town rose. Hundreds upon hundreds of duplex houses were divided straight down the middle, with two rooms upstairs, three rooms downstairs, and half a porch on front and rear for each family. Foundation posts were of black locust; the wooden framing was white oak; the weatherboarding was yellow poplar. Interior walls were of lath and plaster. Fireplaces provided heat, and one room was fitted with a flue for a coal-burning kitchen stove. There were eight hundred of these square, graceless look-alike dwellings, and two hundred smaller single-family cottages. Behind them (except on Lakeside's Silk Stocking Row, where there were furnaces and bathrooms with flush toilets) stood rows of identical privies and coal houses. A generation later the new town would be home to 12,000 people.[16]

Across the ridge another town was going up—McRoberts. It, too, was named for a mogul, Samuel McRoberts, vice-president and executive manager of the Rockefeller-controlled National City Bank of New York. His directorships were legion, including Armour & Company, Union Stock Yards, National Packing Company, American Can Company, American Sugar Refining Company, Continental Bank of Chicago, Baldwin Locomotive Company, Piedmont & Northern Railway, Banque Nationale de la Republique d'Haiti, Bank of the Metropolis of New York City, the Metropolitan Trust Company, and ten life and casualty insurance companies. The exclusivity of his clubs was in keeping with the loftiness of his business connections. With America's entry into World War I a few years later, McRoberts would be commissioned a brigadier general, and his long list of distinctions was topped off in 1918, when he became a chevalier of the French Legion of Honor.[17]

Consol's third town, thirty-five miles distant, was almost a duplicate of McRoberts. It was named Van Lear for old Van Lear Black. (In 1921 this same Van Lear Black, president of the Fidelity and Deposit Company of Maryland, would use his yacht to carry Franklin Delano Roosevelt, vice-president in charge of the firm's New York office, to Campobello, where the young future president was stricken with polio.[18])

While Clarence Watson drove his underlings to build Consol's railroads and towns, he and his associates were putting together another string of huge new communities on the properties of Elk Horn Coal Corporation. Like Consol's towns, these had been launched by Northern Coal & Coke and had been purchased along with the land on which they were rising. Almost identical in size and shape to the ones at Jenkins, Van Lear, and McRoberts, the wooden structures stretched in monotonous and forbidding rows with tipples, ice houses, warehouses, depots, commissaries, and offices interspersed among them. These stark and astonishing towns were also named for moguls: Haymond for Thomas N. Haymond, Fleming for George W. Fleming, and Wayland for Clarence Wayland Watson. Hemphill was consecrated to the memory of Alexander J. Hemphill, chairman of Guaranty Trust Company in New York, whose brokers "moved the paper" of Elk Horn Coal. Wheelwright took its name from Jere Wheelwright, who had become president of Consol. Simultaneously the Mayo-Fairmont syndicate built Weeksbury, a town with a composite name that honored a couple of lesser tycoons.[19]

Even after Clarence Watson moved on to the more rarefied atmosphere of the U.S. Senate, he kept a close grip on the company.[20] He lived for a time at its headquarters in Baltimore, retaining his farm and immense house at Fairmont. Mayo crossed the Big Sandy early in 1911 with a valise loaded with clean shirts and money; he lobbied industriously in Charleston, and in due time the solons of West Virginia recognized Watson's sterling qualities and elected him to the "world's greatest deliberative body." A disgruntled state legislator observed, "It does beat hell how a coal operator from Kentucky came over here and took a millionaire from Maryland and sent him to Washington as a United States Senator from West Virginia!"

Mayo should not be accorded all the credit for turning this mogul into a solon. A West Virginia newspaper reported that the president of Consol arrived in Charleston "armed with a checkbook and a fountain pen." The combination of valise and checkbook proved unbeatable in the eyes of the lawmakers, and Watson, the merger king, expressed his gratitude to the people and their elected representatives for the high honor they had bestowed upon him.[21]

Watson undertook to hold both his senatorial and managerial positions, but soon after he entered the Senate Consol's affairs compelled him to miss a vote on a shipping bill that Pendragon strongly opposed. He demanded that Watson give up one position or the other, and so the senator surrendered his beloved Consol to the capable hands of Jere Wheelwright.[22]

When the rails reached Jenkins and McRoberts, fourteen mines were under development, tipples were rearing up gaunt and graceless, and heaps of glittering coal waited for "gons" to wheel them to market. At Elk Horn Coal's towns the new tipples began to clatter as the rows of houses filled up with men from the construction gangs and endless files of newcomers. The "transportation men," whose passage was paid by the companies in return for covenants to labor until all debts were paid, were not unlike the indentured servants of an earlier day. For ten to fifteen cents per hour they built the "magic towns" (as the newspapers often called them) and poured out the rivers of coal that would make the region famous.

Mayo brought off another tremendous coup in 1906. With funding from Kimberly and the Fairmont ring, he persuaded the state's legislature to tackle the hoary problem of those vexatious Virginia land grants. The bill he advocated passed so quickly and quietly that the heirs of those long-dead revolutionaries suspected nothing until it had been signed into law by the governor. The Revenue Law of 1906 made it the duty of a claimant to pay all taxes which had been or should have been assessed against land for the years 1901-5 and made failure to pay such taxes for any three of those years grounds for a mandatory forfeiture of the title to the Commonwealth, *or to any adverse claimant in actual possession of all or part of the land who had paid such taxes.* The Virginians had, of course, neglected to pay taxes on their ancestral claims, and with this law on the books Mayo's companies computed the delinquent levies and paid them on behalf of their grantors and themselves. Some of the Virginians promptly sued to invalidate the act, but hundreds of heavily armed mountaineers came to the trial and scowled at the judge until he perceived that the law was sound and entered judgment upholding it. On appeal it was sustained by the state's highest court on December 20, 1907.[23] The opinion was written by Chief Justice Edward O'Rear, an ambitious country boy from Camargo in the hills of Montgomery County. After a discreet interval he resigned from the court and became chief counsel in Kentucky for the Consolidation Coal Company. He prospered mightily and bought himself a huge Bluegrass farm in Woodford County, where he ate burgoo and drank bourbon with his neighbor, Johnson Newlon Camden, Jr. Ivan Kimbrell remembered Watson's comment made many years later: "John C. C. got Ed to make us a law that we just had to have!"

Though Mayo had read law and gained admittance to the bar, he never practiced extensively. Still, his legal studies enabled him to draft or acquire the most important legal document in the history of eastern Kentucky—the mineral conveyance known variously to lawyers, judges, and the press as the "Northern," "Mayo," or "broad-form" deed.[24] This court opinion and a copy of the "broad-form" deed should be read by any serious student of Kentucky history. Mayo's work, they are the most important legal documents in the history of Kentucky's eastern counties. With them he swept away the claims of the Virginians, stripped the titles from the native inhabitants, and "vested" the minerals in the new corporate owners. The Virginians were excluded entirely, and the Kentuckians were reduced to little more than tenants by sufferance—people who could use their farms only so long as their presence did not impede mining.

Mayo's forfeiture law was buttressed and reinforced by the election, in 1911, of a marvelously compliant and cooperative governor. Searching for a chief executive who would do their bidding quickly and unhesitatingly, Mayo and the Fairmont ring found him in aged former governor James B. McCreary, who had been out of office and living in well-deserved obscurity for thirty years. At the Sinton Hotel in Cincinnati, Mayo met with Percy Haley of the L&N, Clarence Watson, and Johnson Camden, Jr., to plot McCreary's resurrection. The mystified old man made a sudden and surprising comeback, energetically implementing Mayo's "little forfeiture law." His reward was having a county created and named for him—the last of the state's one hundred and twenty pint-sized principalities. McCreary was so grateful to Mayo that, at the governor's reception dedicating the new state executive mansion, he insisted that the coal magnate stand by his side in the receiving line—king and kingmaker receiving the people's plaudits.

By then Mayo's dreams of riches and power had been realized. He had established himself as a power broker in two states and was Kentucky's member of the Democratic National Committee. He had been offered a U.S. Senate seat and his party's nomination for governor but had rejected both. He had begun the promotional work that would send Johnson Camden, Jr., to the Senate from his adopted state in 1914. He was rich in lands, in corporate stocks, in money, and in public esteem. Although poverty was safely behind him, the memory of poverty lingered. He once showed a friend $200,000 worth of bonds which, he said, represented "cigar money." When he was young he could not afford the luxury of tobacco; those bonds and their coupons guaranteed that he would never again be without the cheering influence of fine Havanas.[25]

In his trips to Baltimore, Fairmont, and New York Mayo had sat as a guest in great houses designed as much to coerce and overawe as to shelter. He vowed to build for himself and Alice a mansion that would eclipse Clarence Watson's LaGrange, J. O. Watson's immense Tudor-style Highgate, George Jenkins's vast stone dwelling, and the awesome splendors of George Fleming at Fairmont and on New York's Fifth Avenue. He would outbuild them all.

Mayo bought a swamp on the fringe of Paintsville and filled it with dirt to make well-drained lawns. He housed a hundred Italian masons in temporary shacks and set them to work with bricks and rooftiles imported from their sunny homeland. They

quarried from the hills the blocks of stone for the foundations
and the wall that enclosed the grounds, and they hauled the materials suspended from a groaning cable to the swarming site.
Eight gigantic carved stone pillars were conveyed on stupendous, specially built ox-drawn wagons to their places in front of
the edifice. The house rose in dark red brick, roofed with inde-
structible tiles and fronted with those breath-taking pillars—a
palace suitable for a coal king at home amid his retainers,
vassals, and allies. The rafters and roof sheathing were sawed
from Kentucky white oak and yellow poplar, and the interior
was paneled and balustraded with yellow oak and exotic ma-
hogany from Honduras. The building stood sixty-six feet wide
and seventy-eight feet long, with porches and balconies, parlors,
reception chambers, a ballroom, conference rooms, a library, a
music chamber, a sewing room, bedrooms, kitchens, dining
rooms, servants' quarters, and (of course) suites for visiting
moguls from near and far.[26] It is doubtful that any comparable
mansion ever towered above Kentucky soil. Here was no ersatz
keep of a Bluegrass tobacco farmer or whiskey distiller, with
hollow wooden columns piteously emulating those carved by
Roman chisels. These were walls of solid brick laid many courses
thick, built to endure for centuries. In scope and grandeur the
building exceeded the habitations of Mayo's fellow moguls at
Fairmont and Baltimore. It proclaimed his status in brick and
stone—successful, secure, powerful, and rich.

The architect measured off wall spaces for canvases and sent
to Rome for appropriate allegorical paintings. In due time they
arrived, gleaming with paint fresh from the artist's brush. They
were placed on the walls of the ballroom—eight of them depict-
ing Mayo's vision of the past and future. The hills stood grim
and forested, shrouded in the silence of the ages. They were sundered by an uprearing titan in freshly broken chains, symbol-
izing the raw, relentless power of Industrialization in a young
and growing nation. The land changed as mills and mines
turned out wealth and people shook off the misery and impotence of poverty and ignorance. Plenty and Peace smiled down
on tranquil, busy, happy, and prosperous valleys.

Mayo did not release his workmen when his mansion stood
complete, its huge and numerous rooms carpeted and furnished.

Red Ash, Whitley County, in the Age of the Moguls. (Alice Lloyd College Archives.)

Street scene in Bellecraft, Letcher County, 1923. (Jennie Darsie Collection, University of Kentucky Archives, Lexington.)

View from above the tipple at the Bellecraft camp, 1923. (Jennie Darsie Collection.)

FOR U. S. SENATOR

CLARENCE W. WATSON

"Wilson Needs Watson"
ELECTION, TUESDAY, NOVEMBER 5

Clarence Wayland Watson, president of Consolidation Coal Company and a candidate for the U.S. Senate, in Lieutenant Colonel's uniform. (West Virginia University Archives, Morgantown.)

Aretas Brooks Fleming, governor of West Virginia and chief counsel of Consolidation Coal Company. (West Virginia University archives.)

Johnson Camden, Jr., U.S. senator from Kentucky and president of Kentucky River Coal Corporation. (Source unknown.)

Coal tipple at Red Ash, Whitley County, ca. 1922. (Alice Lloyd College Archives.)

Rather, he set them to building a new Methodist church a short walk from his mighty door, a place where a mogul could serve his God. At Mayo's request the steel tycoon Andrew Carnegie paid for the organ. Then, a block beyond, Mayo had the workers build the new First National Bank of Paintsville, where a mogul could sequester, command, and serve Mammon. Church and bank bear the imprint of those master masons—staunch, enduring, and singular.

Finally, at a corner of his grounds, they built an office from which Mayo could manage his empire. All of these buildings—mansion, office, church, and bank—stand close together, convenient to the master spirit that created them. Then he laid a railroad track to a short brick-paved street alongside his home, where private railroad cars could be parked when business or pleasure brought the mighty to his door.

Mayo's fortune grew along with his house and temples. He discovered on the waters of the Kentucky River in Letcher, Perry, Breathitt, and Leslie Counties people who were so ignorant and shiftless that they would "sell" their minerals for a mere fifty cents per acre. Mayo joined a new friend, C. Bascom Slemp from Big Stone Gap, Virginia, who had already bought 90,000 acres; they brought in as a partner Johnson Camden, Jr., and purchased the minerals in entire districts. Ever heedful of the need for powerful allies, they recruited two other moguls, an ancient veteran of the Mexican War named John Devall Langhorne (a Washington, D.C., resident who was president of Virginia's Lynchburg Trust & Savings Bank) and his brother Daniel, who were buying minerals for their Tennis Coal Company. They and Slemp brought fresh political muscle to the expanding ring. Slemp was the most influential congressman from his state, a man who had defended state's rights so powerfully and opposed anti-lynching laws so vociferously that he was the darling of Virginia's Old Guard. He was beloved of Standard Oil, too, and helped to enact the Payne-Aldrich tariff of 1909. Slemp was described as a "fluent and delightful conversationalist"—just what Mayo needed to round up those mineral-rich acres for a half-dollar each.[27] (On Jones' Fork in Harlan County, some bumpkins sold out to other tycoons for a mere dime per acre!)

Mayo was planning the formation of another land company to rival Elk Horn Coal in the extent and value of its holdings. Indeed, he was determined to bring *all* the land speculators, old and new, large and small, into a super-merger that would place the gigantic mineral wealth of eastern Kentucky—all 10,600 square miles of it—under a single board of directors. Clarence Wayland Watson would doubtless make a superb president of such a corporate colossus, and its stockholders could find no better choice for chairman of the board than John Caldwell Calhoun Mayo.[28]

By 1914 this new ring of moguls—Mayo, Camden, the Langhornes, Slemp, and the Watsons and Flemings—had acquired title for or binding options to buy nearly 190,000 acres of superb steam coal. Meanwhile, Mayo organized the Mayo Lumber Company to cut virgin timber from his land, and with former West Virginia Governor Justin Collins he established Collins & Mayo Collieries Corporation. By this time the former barefoot woodchopper had become Kentucky's dominant politician, with immense and growing influence in the loftiest financial and political circles of Maryland, Virginia, and West Virginia. He could raise millions from banks in New York, Baltimore, Philadelphia, and Boston. He was on a first-name basis with Roosevelts, Delanos, Forbeses, and several members of the formidable Standard Oil trust, all of whom were major investors in Consolidation Coal and other eastern Kentucky mining firms. A Senate seat or the governor's office remained his for the asking.[29] He told friends that he would found a college at Paintsville for the education of mountain youths.

What did Mayo want? There is some evidence that he was thinking of selling it all—house, bank, lands, corporate stocks—so he could move unencumbered to Brazil or Argentina. The vast ore deposits of the southern continent tantalized him; perhaps he could be the man to build on South American ore a gigantic international steel trust that would dwarf even J. P. Morgan's United States Steel Company.[30] In fact, Mayo had already begun to operate on a continental scale. His Northern Coal & Coke Company hired the infamous Baldwin-Felts detective agency to intervene on behalf of the operators in the embattled coal fields of Colorado, and in 1911 the company sold extensive mineral lands and mining properties there to the Rocky Mountain Fuel Company.[31]

But John Mayo had come to the end of his days. In February, 1914, he became ill at home. Clarence Watson sent his palatial railroad car to carry "John C. C." to New York and the nation's finest specialists. Mayo fought hard for his life, as he had fought for his fortune, but this time he lost. Despite a remarkable new procedure—a blood transfusion from the veins of his brother Washington—he died in a princely suite at the Waldorf-Astoria on May 11, 1914. The cause of his death was listed as pericarditis.[32]

The grandeur of John Mayo's funeral has never been equaled —or even approached—in the history of his state. Clarence Watson's special railway car, draped in black and redolent of flowers, brought him home. All of Kentucky's state-level elected officials went to Paintsville in a chartered train loaded with mourners. Watson arrived with sixty bankers and officials of his companies. Mayo's honorary pallbearers included Kentucky's governor, a former governor and a senator, Congressman Slemp, both senators from West Virginia, the president of the nation's biggest coal company, the president of the Louisville & Nashville Railroad, and Mayo's faithful and beloved friend John Buckingham. There were so many moguls that the huge, solemn special trains with their luxurious private cars could find no parking space; the railroad tycoons stopped coal shipments for several hours while the gleaming locomotives and visitors' coaches stood in line on the main track. No greater tribute could have been paid to a coal king than to bring the rumbling "drags" to a halt in his honor.

An eloquent minister was imported from Louisville, and the church was so crowded that even the standing room was taken and an immense, somber crowd filled the streets. The poor, too, paid their respects—including many who had been made much poorer by the sale of their mineral riches. On the day before the funeral they passed the body in silent hundreds, staring at Mayo's immobile features and looking around with startled, uncomprehending gazes at the splendid rooms.

In a funeral tribute Clarence Watson summed up the feeling of an age about this strange, compelling man:

His abilities were such that he made the skeptics see, as he saw, the inexhaustible riches sealed in those remote hills, and he changed the men who laughed at this faith into enthusiastic converts to his plan. Through all those years he worked . . . without rest, to develop eastern Kentucky along the large and lofty lines of his prophetic visions. He was an empire builder, as were Clive and Rhodes and Hill and McKenzie, and what was done by these great men for India and South Africa, for our great Northwest and for Canada's imperial domain, John Mayo did for Eastern Kentucky. He possessed all of the mental attributes of the great empire builder. He could see the harvest ere the grain was sown, and on the mid-night sky of rain could paint the golden morrow.[33]

In other words, he had brought to the Kentucky mountains a colonialism such as English conquerors had imposed on the lands and peoples of Africa.

Practically every newspaper in Kentucky and many in other states reported Mayo's death and editorialized about his accomplishments. The *Big Sandy News* devoted its entire front page and half of another to him and his works. The *New York Times* said he was the wealthiest man in his state, with a net worth of $20 million.

Mayo was buried on a hilltop above the valley of Levisa Fork. An immense stone patterned after the tomb of Napoleon bears the word "Mayo," and a flat slab tells his name and the dates of his birth and death. The rains of many autumns have watered his grave, and the man so honored and respected in his lifetime lies forgotten. For some incomprehensible reason nearly all Kentucky historians have omitted him from their volumes.

Perhaps Mayo's ghost sometimes meets that of Alexander Arthur, the doughty Scot who built Middlesborough at Cumberland Gap and who sank into poverty when the giant bubble burst. In their phantom musings they may wonder at the meanings of their strange careers.

SEVEN

The Kingdom of Lynch

Southeast of the Kentucky hill country lie the Kentucky mountains—the long, broken escarpments of the Cumberland and Pine, and the tangled, somber ridges of the Big and Little Black. In this labyrinth the state has its greatest rainfall and its loftiest elevations. Here grew the largest white oaks, black walnuts, and yellow poplars of Kentucky's fabled forest.

This land between Cumberland Gap and Flat Gap is without passes; the pioneers shunned it as almost impenetrable. Streams tumbled down to rocky creeks that were hard to ford. It required a day for an agile man to climb the Black Mountain and come down again. Buffaloes had worn broad trails through the gaps, but the game paths in this heartland were almost indiscernible. Tangles of wild "cane" choked the narrow valleys and strove to crush mammoth sycamores that were sometimes fifteen feet thick. The sixty-million-year-old forest was an interlocked jungle of hard and soft woods. Scores of acres were overrun with laurel and rhododendron thickets that only a snake or chipmunk could penetrate. Where lightning had set fires, groves of saplings blocked the way of any hunter seeking bear and deer. The ferns, ginseng, and wildflowers that carpeted the forest floor hid dens of deadly copperheads and rattlesnakes. Even the best woodsman could get lost in such a place, meet injury, and leave his corpse to the buzzards.

Something else lay in those huge tumbled ridges between the Cumberland and Pine Mountains: coal, many veins of it, some much higher than a tall man, and rich with the stored heat of lost aeons.

Writing nearly a century ago, James Lane Allen described the mineral treasure, the barriers defending it, and the great gaps that opened like gates to admit pioneers and industrialists in their turn:

> On the Kentucky side of the mighty wall of the Cumberland Mountain, and nearly parallel with it, is the sharp single wall of the Pine Mountain, the westernmost ridge of the Allegheny system. For about a hundred miles these two gnarled and ancient monsters lie crouched side by side guarding an immense valley of timbers and irons and coals. Near the middle point of this inner wall there occurs a geological fault. The mountain falls apart as though cut in twain by some heavy downward stroke, showing on the faces of the fissure precipitous sides wooded to the crests. There is thus formed the celebrated and magnificent pass through which the Cumberland River—one of the most beautiful in the land—slips silently out of its mountain valley and passes on to the hills and the plateaus of Kentucky.[1]

A tradition relates that a lone Virginian named Joseph Martin, seeking out lands for a syndicate that included Patrick Henry, wandered into the place before Boone blazed the Wilderness Trail. He found wild clover growing along a stream and left behind two names—Martin's Fork and Clover Fork. In time, a settler named Looney hewed out a clearing at the south base of the Big Black, and his son ventured across the peak and cleared a corn patch on a stream, later known as Looney Creek, that flowed down toward the north and west.

The people who inhabited this rich core of the Kentucky Cumberlands when the twentieth century began carried about a dozen family names—Ledford, Middleton, Smith, Skidmore, Caywood, Asher, Howard, Noe, Turner, Hensley, Napier, and Farmer. They were the descendants of Aley Ledford, James Farmer, and Noble Smith, who had surveyed a stupendous boundary of about 190,000 acres in the 1840's. Their title to the land was dubious for several technical reasons, but in 1876 Edward Davis of Philadelphia learned about their claim and sent lawyers to Harlan to see whether it could be bought. They decided that 86,000 acres could be acquired with reasonable certainty of title, and Davis made the purchase for $86,000.[2] There the matter rested until 1902, when Franklin D. Roosevelt's uncle, Warren Delano, Jr., was elected to the boards of the

Louisville & Nashville and its parent, the Atlantic Coastline Railroad. Being privy to the railroad's intention to build lines into the country, he organized a syndicate to straighten out the remaining title problems and secure the mineral rights. In a series of trips the jovial Delano overcame all difficulties concerning a large portion of the Davis purchase. By nearly a hundred deeds he cleared the "clouds" from at least 75,000 acres. The land thus secured lay mainly in Kentucky, with lesser areas in Tennessee and Virginia.

The purchasing syndicate included Delano, Edward Davis's son Charles, a Roosevelt or two, and (as petty shareholders) some three dozen ambitious and hard-bitten local lawyers, merchants, and politicians, including Lee Ball, Arthur Cornett, George W. Green, Hamp Howard, John White Farmer, Marion Smith, Will W. Noe, and Will Ward Duffield. In 1907 Delano organized the Kentenia Corporation, to which the mineral rights and extensive fee-simple holdings were conveyed. He remained on the boards of the two railroad companies until 1920 and early in his tenure saw tracks laid to the heart of Kentenia's holdings on Puckett's Creek and Catron's Creek. There Kentenia built mining towns and commenced producing coal.

The name of this corporate mineral fiefdom was created by borrowing a syllable from the name of each of the three states— Kentucky, Tennessee, and Virginia—in which its domain lay. Its headquarters were at South Yarmouth, Massachusetts, where a relief map of "the Kentenia Country" hung above the paneled walls and Persian carpets of the board room. The corporation was capitalized at $10 million, of which $4.25 million worth of the stock was issued at the outset to "Delano and Davis" and $2 million more to Davis alone.

Young Franklin Delano Roosevelt sometimes accompanied his uncle on trips to Harlan and helped with the title work in the courthouse. Like Delano, he was a charmer, and he was warmly welcomed to the gossip sessions around the stoves in the county-seat stores. He amazed the assembled tobacco chewers by the elegant manner in which he spat between his front teeth—a skill some of the young men emulated.[3] In June, 1908, he wrote a series of letters to his wife, Eleanor, in which he informed her of conditions in Kentucky:

Pennington Gap, Va.
Friday Evening
June 12th, '08

The letter head will explain to you where we are just as well as
I could without the aid of a map. Suffice it to say that we are
spending the night here, having arrived at 9:30 p.m. We are in the
point of Virginia which runs down to where Kentucky and Tennessee join. Tomorrow we leave at 7 a.m., take the train down the
valley about 20 miles to a place called Hagan, get our horses
there and ride over the mountains over Boone's trail to Harlan in
Kentucky, our headquarters. Next Thursday night we come out
to the R.R. at Pinesville, far to the S.W. of this, take train on Friday to Knoxville, Tenn., and get to Washington some time on
Sunday . . . the trip today has been so wonderful to me that I
can't begin to tell you about it now. We woke up near Hagers-
town, Maryland, and ever since have been coming through wonderful valleys and hills. In some places we were over 2,000 feet
up, and the train ran thro gorges that for sheer beauty beat anything that we saw in the Black Forest.

Pennington Gap, Va.
Monday Morning
June 15

This letter head is erroneous as to our location, as we have
come many miles into the mountains, staying at Mr. Henry
Smith's house about three miles from Harlan.

We got up on Saturday morning at Pennington at 6 a.m. took
the train about 18 miles down the valley to Hagan and found the
horses waiting at the station. We had been joined by a Mr. Whiteley of Baltimore, the manager of some iron mines just South of
Hagan and we rode down the railway as far as the mines and
came to the path running into Kentucky over the Cumberland
Mountains which Daniel Boone came over on his first Westward
journey. If you can imagine a succession of ridges, each fifteen
hundred or so feet above the valleys, running up at a very pre-
cipitous angle and covered with marvelous trees and an under-
growth of rhododendrons and holly you can get a general idea of
the country—the path was just about the steepest kind that I
would care to take a horse up, following generally a water course
filled with boulders and ledges of rock. We formed a cavalcade of
five, Mr. Whiteley, Mr. Wolf, the superintendent of the Boone's

Path Iron Co., Uncle Warren, Mr. Lowell, W. D.'s local attorney, and me. My horse is small, but wiry and sure footed. Uncle Warren rode a mule, as the horse intended for him had a sore back.

We got to the top of the Cumberland Mountain about 10 o'clock and had one of the most magnificent views I have ever seen, looking to the south over the angle of Virginia almost to the mountains of North Carolina and Tennessee, and to the Northward over the Harlan County, Kentucky, section that Uncle Warren and Davis are interested in. We continued along the ridge for a mile or so, got lost, came over the top and started down into the valley over what they thought was a trail. I thought otherwise— for half an hour we slipped, slid and fell down the slope, the horses slipping, sliding and almost falling on top of us, and ended up in a heap in the stream at the bottom. Uncle Warren said it was about the roughest ride he has ever had here. We rode N. E. along the creek about five or six miles, when Mr. Whiteley and Wolf left us to recross the ridge to their mine. We had some chocolate and spring water for lunch, at 2 o'clock, then started up over Black Mountain on a so-called wagon road—positively the worst road I have ever seen or imagined and one which was not really easy to traverse on horseback. We dropped down into the valley along Catron's Creek and came to this house at about 6:30, having done 22 or 23 miles in all, most of it on the roughest trail and worst road in a county famous throughout the land for bad trails and worse roads.'

This house belongs to Mr. Henry Smith, about the most prosperous farmer of the county and his bottomlands along the valley are splendid. I must close this long epistle hurriedly as the mail is going. Will add this p.m.

Harlan
Monday, p.m.

I had to close abruptly my last missive as the mail decided to start out to the railroad a little ahead of time. I will take this up where I left off.

On Sunday we breakfasted very late at Mr. Smith's, 7 o'clock, and sat around for an hour, discussing legal and political affairs, and soon after rode in to Harlan, about 3½ miles, which means about 7 miles anywhere else, because of the horrible conditions of the roads here.

On arrival at Harlan we were met by Mr. Duffield, the man-

ager of Kentenia, and by most of the famous men of the town—
sat around "chewing the rag," lunched at the Imperial Hotel,
which is conducted by the County Judge, Judge Lewis. He and
his wife do all the work and he waits on table. He is 29 only and
they have been married 15 years and have two children.

We climbed to the top of the small hill close to the town and
rode back to Smith's after a severe thunderstorm. Last night I sat
up till eleven discussing law with Mr. Lowell, and was up at 6 this
morning.

We rode into Harlan again in time for lunch and are now en-
sconced here, saddle bags and all, at Judge Lewis' Hotel. This
afternoon we are just back from a ride of five or six miles up
Martin Fork, the most beautiful country we have seen yet. The
sides of the valley going up 2,000 feet, heavily wooded with great
poplars, chestnuts and a dozen or two other deciduous trees and
every mile or so a fertile bottom with fine crops and a stream of
splendid water. I will add to this in the morning.

Tuesday. Can't add, just off for an all-day ride up Clover Fork.[4]

The president-to-be wore a woolen sweater marked with a
huge Harvard H, doubtless the first insignia of that campus to
enter the Kentucky hills, and astounded the lethargic mountaineers with the zestful leapfrog jumps by which he bounded
onto the back of his horse.

On one of his Harlan County expeditions FDR met James
Otis Watson II, who was buying mineral lands for the Fairmont
ring. The ring acquired 8,000 acres of Harlan land and a lasting
friendship with young Roosevelt and his uncle. The Watsons
and Roosevelt were attracted to one another by similarity of
background and political affiliation.[5]

Kentenia leased coal lands to other newly formed mining
companies. Suddenly Harlan County, long an inert backwoods,
became a hive of activity as railroads were built, spur lines were
extended up a score of valleys, and entire towns were planned
and constructed. Most of them were squalid, underfinanced
camps thrown together hastily by fly-by-night operators who
hoped to get rich in the impending coal boom and decamp to
other regions.[6] However, some of the new communities were
quite good when viewed in the context of their age. The best
were built by Kentenia and by International Harvester, which
had acquired 6,000 acres near the mouth of Looney Creek.

Grading for pit mouth, main heading, south side of Looney Creek, Lynch, January 28, 1918. (Charles A. Billips Collection, Lexington, Ky.)

Builders of Lynch, Appalachia's most ambitious coal town. (Charles A. Billips Collection.)

Lynch under construction, October 1, 1919. (Charles A. Billips Collection.)

Coal Miners' Hotel, Lynch, February 1, 1919. The building has since been demolished. (Charles A. Billips Collection.)

When Henry Ford undertook to build an integrated industrial empire of lumber, rubber, paint, coal, and steel to supply his automobile factories, he turned to eastern Kentucky and bought more than 50,000 acres in Letcher, Pike, Harlan, and Leslie Counties. Out of affection for his son Edsel he called the Kentucky holding company Fordson. Its Banner Fork Mining Company, which was acquired in 1920 and worked out and abandoned in 1931, was deemed a model of planning, construction, advanced mining technology, and corporate paternalism.[7]

The coal boom that so shook and altered the hills was given a surge of new power and breadth by the outbreak of war in Europe. The beleaguered allies needed steel for guns, ships, engines, trucks, and (after 1916) tanks. They needed explosives, too, and the Harlan coal was rich in toluol, a hydrocarbon that was helping to pound entire provinces. Even before the United States entered the war, the county was in the throes of an indescribable tempest. Wages were astronomical. Twenty mining towns were being put together, roads were being blasted out of hillsides, rails were being spiked to oak ties, tipples were being bolted into place, and tunnels were penetrating innumerable mountain slopes. Engulfed by the tumult, the hill people rushed into the camps. Their "arrested frontier culture" underwent cyclonic change as the county's population zoomed from 10,556 in 1910 to 31,546 in 1920.[8] Besides mining coal, they drank whiskey from the numerous moonshine stills and fought with pistols, knives, and Winchesters. In 1916 the homicide rates in Letcher and Harlan Counties were the highest in America, 77.9 and 63.5 per 100,000 population respectively. "Bloody Harlan" acquired its deadly reputation long before the infamous labor wars of the 1930's.[9]

Americans love "crash programs," of which World War II's Manhattan Project and the moon race of the 1960's are prime examples. Private businesses often launch similar crash programs, as exemplified by the construction of transcontinental railroads after the Civil War. These efforts are undertaken in an atmosphere of extreme anxiety and are pushed to consummation with scant concern for cost. In such a situation the end is deemed to justify practically any means, and the consequences can be spectacular.

The development of the large-scale coal industry in the upper reaches of the Cumberland, Kentucky, and Big Sandy valleys was brought off in the heady atmosphere of a mammoth capitalistic "rush." A mighty war was about to engulf the world, and the need for coal (and the corresponding profits) promised to be immense. The tracks were laid, the mines were sunk, the towns were built, and the workmen were found within a tiny fraction of the time ordinarily required for projects of such scope. So rapidly did the industrial world overwhelm Harlan County that in a mere eight years (1911-18) coal production increased from 1,440 to 3,201,733 tons, while the number of miners went from 169 to 4,123.

America's declaration of war against the Central Powers in April, 1917, set off tremendous activity in the offices and mills of United States Steel. Assembled by J. P. Morgan in 1901, it was the nation's largest corporation; during World War II it would pour more steel than all the Axis Powers combined. It enjoyed abundant financing through its Morgan connections, and it had other gargantuan lines of credit available. Pendragon had sold to Morgan's immense steel combine the Mesabi iron range that he had acquired from the luckless Merritt brothers for a mere $500,000. For this rich property he was paid $80,000,000, half in common stocks and half in preferred. These developments made him the largest non-corporate shareholder in U.S. Steel and gave him a seat on its board.[10]

It is almost impossible for an American president to develop the prestige and will necessary for a successful confrontation with a major industry. Politicians are usually small-town lawyers who wield power for a while and then go home. By contrast, industrialists and financiers have lifetime tenure, and successors may perpetuate their policies. It should not surprise us, then, that during World War I U.S. Steel sold armor plate to Russia and Italy for $349 and $395 per ton respectively, then sold the same product to the United States for $604! With such a conveyor belt leading from the United States Treasury to their own ample vaults, the directors of "Big Steel" were eager to increase production vastly and quickly. The corporation's profits on "war orders" eventually reached $889,931,000—a sum equal to the par value of all its stock.[11] (This magnificent achievement was brought off under a "liberal" and "progressive" federal administration that paid its privates less than seventy cents a day for attacking German machine gun nests.)

America's involvement lasted only nineteen months, but the war's quick end could not have been anticipated in April, 1917. The struggle had raged for nearly three years and Germany had proved itself a ferocious and cunning foe. Italy had been battered into quiescence. The French were benumbed by more than a million battle deaths, and the submarine blockade had brought the British to the brink of starvation. Russia had given up entirely; Belgium was occupied and helpless. Germany's eastern armies were shifting to the west and her factories, given a breathing spell, were turning out floods of new weapons. The armies that had won these victories were likely to last a long time. It was with this in mind that U.S. Steel sent one of its ablest metallurgical engineers, L. A. Billips, in search of an abundant deposit of top-quality coal. He looked at a number of other fields but found what he wanted on Looney Creek, east of International Harvester's spic-and-span new town of Benham. Into the bedlam of town, tipple, and railroad construction that was Harlan County, Kentucky, the immense steel trust—so recently a target of President William Howard Taft's trust-busters—thrust itself with almost immeasurable energy.[12]

Billips found three veins in the Big Black, all of the coal good and most of it excellent for steel-making. Tests revealed it to be low in ash, moisture, and sulphur and high in volatile matter. Its coke oven gases were rich in toluol. Best of all, perhaps, there was a single tract of the coal of proven title and held by a single owner, the Wentz Corporation of Philadelphia; 14,405 acres contained many hundreds of millions of tons of fuel. Because the Louisville & Nashville terminated only three miles down the creek from the site Billips thought suitable for town and mine, it would not require years of hassling with railroaders to obtain the necessary access.

On August 4, 1917, U.S. Steel committed itself to an immense enterprise where, until recently, only a few isolated farmers had lived. The Wentz Corporation property was bought forthwith, and agents hastened to buy additional tracts.[13] (By the early 1930's the company owned 30,000 acres, holdings that

have since grown by an additional 11,000 acres.) The land secured, the corporation pushed the project with all possible
speed, employing its own men and talents. The greatest industrial organization then in existence anywhere on earth needed
no contractors and subcontractors. The town that rose and the
complex that necessitated it were entirely the products of the
Rockefeller-Morgan behemoth, with the construction actually
done by a wholly owned subsidiary, U.S. Coal & Coke.

Men were set to work grading a road from Benham three
miles upstream, where the mountains drew apart somewhat to
reveal a bit of bottomland. Trainloads of supplies arrived and
were hauled on wagons and feeble trucks to the construction
site. Everything had to be imported—men, mules, wagons and
more wagons, horses, harnesses, and tools. The latter require-
ment alone was breathtaking; needs had to be anticipated and
then met with loads of hammers, hatchets, axes, post-hole dig-
gers, crowbars, screw drivers, measuring rules, squares, chisels,
shovels, wheelbarrows, picks, and mattocks. The task required
hundreds of stonecutters and brickmasons, carpenters, and
hod-carriers. Cement had to be secured and delivered. Nails
would be required by the ton and in every size from huge spikes
to slender finishing nails, plus many carloads of roofing, lumber,
doors, windows, locks, sashes, tar, paint, paint thinner, and kerosene. They would need thousands of horse and mule shoes and
nails, plus smiths and shops to shape and fit them. The lumber
would include beams, two-by-fours, joists, sills, sheathing,
lathing, and weatherboarding. Nothing could be omitted;
everything had to be anticipated, or hopeless snarls would ensue. And all the necessary items had to be manufactured or
bought in an exploding wartime economy.

While the plans for a new and model town of a thousand residences were being developed in sessions that sometimes lasted
around the clock, the corporation was building its three-mile
railroad from Benham. (The tiny line carried the humble name
of the Looney Creek Railroad.) U.S. Steel could build the track
while the L&N's bureaucracy was pondering the matter.

The town conceived by the Morgan-Rockefeller architects
and sociologists was an example of advanced corporate paternalism. Because there was enough coal to last more than a cen-

tury, everything had to be durable. Labor peace and domestic contentment were essential for such a prolonged operation, so the town would have to be pleasant and the workmen happy. Lynch would be a citadel of peace, order, and productivity.

The plans called for sound houses on lots large enough to assure a reasonable degree of privacy. The plastered interior walls and asbestos slate roofs were palatial extravagances by Appalachian standards. The plans included a water system that could deliver 50 gallons daily per person *inside* each household. The wives of these miners would not have to carry pails from wells to kitchens and bathtubs. For that matter, Lynch miners would not have to go wearily homeward covered with pit grime to take a bath in a tub of water heated on a kitchen stove. Instead, a huge bathhouse with hundreds of showers would send them to their wives clean, shampooed, and refreshed.

Visitors who came to Lynch on business (and simply to see the fantastic success of the place) would stay at a hotel containing 133 spacious, carpeted, steam-heated rooms.

The schools would be strictly segregated, of course, as Kentucky law required; but they would be clean, solidly built, and spacious. Concrete sidewalks would converge on them from every part of town so that children who had plodded through streams and mud puddles to get to the country schools could now reach the company's classrooms with dry feet. There would be grade and high schools, with well-qualified teachers. Paved streets would extend throughout the community so that miners could acquire and use automobiles. A company service station would dispense gasoline and tires. The store would be the largest coal company commissary ever built—a forbidding three-story mercantile fortress, divided into departments like comparable establishments in big cities. Only goods of high quality would be stocked, and prices would allow a modest profit.

The mines would be the most modern in the world, adequately ventilated and electrically lighted throughout. Safety would be the prime consideration from the first shovelful. The coal would pass through a gigantic tipple of steel and cement, the largest and most efficient in the world. The electric power for mine and town would come from a generating plant fueled by Taggart coal.

On Sundays men and their families could go (scrubbed, well dressed, and grateful) to the churches of their choice, for those, too, would be provided by the company: Catholic (Roman and Greek), Methodist, Presbyterian, and Baptist. The company would subsidize the salaries of ministers sound in social and biblical doctrine, as it would support teachers who taught the advantages of a blessed trio—Patriotism, Americanism, and Capitalism.

On the hill overlooking the town would rise a refuge for healing the sick and broken. With thick stone walls constructed by Italian and Hungarian masons would stand a sixty-room hospital, the best in the American coal fields.

The community would be an idyllic place for both workmen and employers. The thick coal veins and solid tops assured working situations in which men could stand up and move freely about, while fans pushed in rivers of air to flush out methane and pumps sucked out any water that accumulated in the "dips." Decent wages and quality goods would foster sound nutrition and respectable appearance. An advanced system of "sani-sept" toilets, the hospital, and a team of visiting nurses promised a clean community and healthy inhabitants. The schools and churches would bring education, faith, and understanding to a conglomerate population.[14]

Lynch would be no democracy. People of similar backgrounds would live together on streets set aside for their particular ethnic group. Everything would be company owned—every brick, stone, and shingle. All except the workmen, managers, and their families could be declared trespassers at the company's pleasure. There would be no communism or radicalism at Lynch because there would be no need for them; in this worker's paradise contentment, not agitation, would reign. There would be no labor unions, because enlightened company policy would give more than any union could hope to gain.

Steel's pay policy was a simple one: all expenses incurred by the miner would be secured in the form of payroll deductions—rent, store accounts, electricity, water, health care. Scrip would be issued, redeemable at the store, service station, restaurant, and "recreation clubs." The balance could be deposited in a company bank so that savings could grow and habits of thrift take root.

Not even the managerial genius and money of the Morgan-Rockefeller empires could execute such an enormous scheme before the armistice on November 11, 1918, but the superintendents accomplished an incredible amount within that brief period. Frank Kearns came to Lynch as its first superintendent but was struck down by the devastating influenza epidemic of 1918. He was succeeded by a brilliant twenty-six-year-old industrial manager named E. V. Albert, who kept the post until the job was finished. Under Albert's steady, unrelenting guidance a vast industrial installation arose from the chaos that had descended on Looney Creek, and an amazing new town was born.

As at Middlesboro and Jenkins in earlier years, the first objective had to be completion of flimsy temporary shelters for the workmen, along with bathing facilities, kitchens, mess halls, and privies. As these necessities were completed and staffed, the labor recruiters began to deliver their gangs. The first consisted of several hundred Italians and Hungarians who began quarrying rocks for foundations, the hospital, store, bathhouse, and retaining walls. The stones were wagoned to the preselected sites, where other gangs cemented them into place.

As the rows of foundations and chimneys took shape, stacks of lumber arrived. Since the architects knew precisely what each house would contain, most of the wood was delivered in the form of precut patterns. A construction foreman directed "framing" carpenters who nailed up the skeleton of the house, put down the flooring, and attached the weatherboarding and roof sheathing. Crews of roofers moved onto the housetops, while lathers nailed narrow wooden strips to the studding and overhead timbers. These were dogged by door and window setters, plasterers, and painters.

Other crews used mules and primitive scrapers to drag away dirt and rock excavated by hundreds of men with picks and shovels. These long, smooth strips were covered with creek gravel, compacted with heavy rollers, and covered with some of the most enduring concrete streets and sidewalks in America. More than ten miles of paved streets and twenty miles of sidewalks went into the emerging city. So rapidly did the project advance that the hotel, begun on June 15, was under roof by the beginning of November. Work on the enormous store commenced in April, 1918, and the structure stood complete the following February. (Some important functions had to be crudely improvised in the commotion. For example, Lynch's first school was located under a huge, overhanging cliff or "rock house" from which two shiftless families were ejected.)

Incredibly, mine shafts were driven during the same few months and in November, 1917, they produced 5,486 tons of precious coal. Less than six years later the Lynch tipple would deliver more than 7,000 tons in one day.

When the war ended, the project was an immense unfinished scar—a jumble of men, draft animals, finished and unfinished houses, heaps of quarried stone, stacks of lumber and bricks, and soil well drenched with sweat. While the pace slowed a little, the moguls did not stop until their masterpiece stood complete. In 1925 the last of the construction crews laid down their tools. Steel's new town was finished.

Four hundred duplexes and two hundred single-residence cottages lined the streets, and a couple of dozen larger and more elegant buildings looked down from secluded neighborhoods located on the cool, shady heights. Here the managers, physicians, and engineers lived on salaries the miners regarded as princely. These houses contained eight to twelve rooms, whereas five rooms were specified for each miner and his family. There were five immense porch-lined boardinghouses for the numerous unmarried men. The town had a railroad station and depot, a fire station with brightly painted red trucks, and a water system that placed each house within no more than 200 feet of a fire hydrant. An automobile road scarred the Big Black, leading to another new town called Appalachia, Virginia. The population was the most cosmopolitan in the state, with Italians, Hungarians, Germans, Austrians, Poles, Greeks, Croats, Russians, Albanians, and a few Bulgarians. Nearly half the residents were what the Constitution quaintly calls "natural born" white Americans, while the remainder were blacks and Europeans. The four main groupings—Northern whites, mountain whites, blacks, and immigrants—could be almost endlessly divided into cultural and linguistic subgroups. In 1920 the population reached 9,200, probably edging up to 10,000 or thereabouts in the mid-1920's, given the high birthrate.

Mining populations are notoriously unstable, as illustrated by the 1920–21 school enrollment records. The fifth and sixth grades began with 61 students, had 52 withdrawals, and ended the year with 82! Nor did the company achieve its goal of a calm, stable, peace-loving adult population. The residents were too young, diverse, and quick tempered for that. There were fights, knifings, shootings, and much drinking. Once a crowd of 1,500 attempted to "rescue" a cache of home-brewed beer from a band of destructive U.S. prohibition officers.

Lynch may have brought off its cultural coup in 1922, when Tina Pattiera, the world-famous Yugoslav tenor, sang at the Croatian Club. He made only one other appearance in the state, at Louisville. In 1927 Italo Picchi of the Metropolitan Opera arrived to sing for the Italians. The black bands drew the biggest crowds, however, with gospel singing and jazz. The community loved sports, and the different ethnic groups took immense pride in players from their own backgrounds. Games often ended in squabbles and brawls with fans from other towns.

The company valued education more than did the surrounding county. In 1928–29 there were thirteen black teachers and at least twice as many whites. The latter received an average salary of $1,100, a high wage for the time. Black teachers were paid more modestly—an average of $800.[15]

The town's day of glory came on February 12, 1923, when the Lynch mine broke the world record for a one-day output of coal at a single operation. There were, on that memorable day, 1,476 men on the payroll, of whom 1,050 worked underground. Eighty-three operated undercutting machines and electric locomotives, while 553 loaded coal onto the cars with shovels. The others included track-layers, timber-setters, pumpers, electricians, and brattice men. They produced 7,089 tons—or 4.8 tons per employee.

Lynch was the first fully electrified coal mine in America, with lights strung to the last cut. The fine coal or "bug dust" clawed out by the undercutting machines—two hundred tons of it daily—went to the powerhouse as fuel and came back as elec-

tricity for the lights, cutting machines, and narrow-gauge subterranean railroads.

Time and technological progress would render the tonnage
modest and the methods primitive, but the town and the moguls
celebrated their feat together. Ironically, though, the swarms of
machine operators, engine drivers, slate pickers and shovelers
were never able to dig enough coal to use the gigantic tipple and
dumphouses to their capacity. They were built to process 15,000
tons daily—a rail gondola every two minutes—but the tunnels
never yielded more than two-thirds of that. This installation and
its drop pits contained 11,000 tons of steel, as much as a fully
armed World War II battle cruiser.

On Lynch's "blue ribbon day" stored coal brought the tonnage loaded onto L&N cars to 10,293. Two hundred ninety-
three working places were undercut. The loaders average 12.25
tons and filled 230 railroad cars—a train 1.65 miles long.[16]

Lynch managers competed for years with those at Clarence
Watson's Jenkins, forty miles away, in their quest for ever higher
one-day outputs. The advantage lay with Steel. Consol had
fourteen tipples servicing scattered operations; no matter how
hard they strove, the men at Jenkins could never send as much
coal through them as clattered each day through the Lynch colossus. Eventually Jenkins would surpass Lynch in overall population and number of employees, but it never produced coal in
such abundance or with such efficiency.[17]

Lynch was built, and operated in its heyday, as a self-contained fiefdom—a little kingdom owned, policed, and operated
by the Morgan-Rockefeller moguls. There was no mayor or
town council, no sheriff or shop steward. "The company"—
that compelling, overriding, all-dominating presence—did everything that people ordinarily do for themselves in a democratic society. The men needed only to work, the women to keep
their houses clean and to cook, the children to study, the teachers to instruct. Company police enforced the law, both corporate and public. The company maintained the independent
school district that ran the schools. The company cared for the
sick. The company undertaker buried the dead. The company-
approved preachers proclaimed the Holy Gospel as conceived
and approved by—the company. And if a man shed his docility

and became "ungrateful," the company police removed his possessions from his company house and conveyed them in a company truck to a point safely beyond the company's property line. If the workman deemed this high-handed and appealed to a court, his case was heard by a judge whose election had been secured by company influence and money. It was all very medieval—and efficient.[18]

Lynch was abundantly policed by a band of no-nonsense cops, and law and order were built into the very substance of the town. After all, Pendragon was a born-again Baptist, and Morgan was a dedicated Episcopalian. These moguls and their fellows in Big Steel were perfectly willing to bankrupt a competitor or turn a profit of millions by selling watered stock to widows, but they were staunchly opposed to minor sins. Even Charles Schwab, perhaps the ablest steel man in U.S. history, was out of the president's office soon after the press reported that he had gambled at Monte Carlo while vacationing in Europe. Gambling and marital infidelity indicated an instability of character that the moguls would not accept.[19]

The place was named for Thomas Lynch, who was born at Uniontown, Pennsylvania, in 1854 and who began his career as a clerk for the coal and coke tycoon, Henry Clay Frick. Frick recognized Lynch's talents as a manager and made him superintendent of his company store at Broadford. Advancement was steady, and at thirty-six Lynch became general manager of Frick Coal & Coke. When Frick retired to New York to collect paintings and live the good life, Lynch succeeded him as president. In due time the Frick companies were bought by U.S. Steel, and Lynch was appointed to head all the coal and coke enterprises of that gargantuan new combine. He took time from his duties with Big Steel to serve as a director of the Union Trust Company, Union Savings Bank, National Bank of Scottdale, the Fayette National Bank, and (more majestic than all the others combined) the Mellon National Bank. If one needed a loan in Pittsburgh, Thomas Lynch was clearly a good man to know.

Lynch moved in elegant society. His memberships included the Duquesne, Greensburg, and Pittsburgh Country Clubs, the Westmoreland Hunt Club, and the Polo Club of Pittsburgh. He was a trustee of the Carnegie Hero Fund and a soundly conservative Republican. Like George C. Jenkins, he was a Roman Catholic and "contributed generously to its many and varied charities."

Lynch has been called the "Father of Mine Safety" in America. In an age when knowledge of mining dangers—weak top, coal dust, methane—were imperfectly understood, he strove to prevent another Monongah. He devised rules of safety which were exceedingly stringent for his time, fired the lackadaisical and careless, and developed a system of rewards for workmen whose "sections" suffered no accidents. His motto survives deep in the concrete portals above long-abandoned entries along Kentucky's Looney Creek: "Safety the First Consideration." [20] He was also an organizer of the Pennsylvania Coal and Iron Police, and a highly skilled union buster. He died in 1914, three years before Morgan and Rockefeller started building the town named after him.

How much did it cost—the houses, churches, boarding-houses, offices, machine shops, power plant, tipples, dump drops, scale houses, hospital, store, streets, sidewalks, water plant, septic facilities, bathhouse, railroad, depot, schools, and mines? We do not know, but in 1925 the company listed its value as $5,774,000. It is a safe bet that Big Steel would not have sold its coal seams alone for five times that figure. A conservative estimate for the entire investment is $25,000,000— and that at a time when a miner paid $8.00 a month rent, $1.60 for household electricity, and $.75 for water.

As an industrial accomplishment the town of Lynch was a marvel, but as a place to live and work it was somehow out of joint from the beginning. It bore a somber and foreboding aura that it could never shake off. The valley is so narrow that the mountains, towering nearly 3,000 feet, are overpowering in their immensity and nearness. They shoulder out the light until the sun is high in the sky, and they bring early shade in the afternoon. The stone walls of the huge buildings are as grim as prisons. Everything is too ordered, preordained, and subdued; the eye of Big Steel is too pervasive. Spontaneity never felt at home there. Lynch was designed by engineers and was as utilitarian and artless as a sledgehammer.

EIGHT

The Rich and Mighty Capitalists

THE APPALACHIAN COAL MINERS' struggle for the right to organize unions and draw decent wages is legendary. It began before the Civil War and continued into the 1930's, when laws pushed by Franklin Delano Roosevelt secured for American workmen the right to collective bargaining and a decent (or at least a minimum) wage.

From Carnegie to Rockefeller, Jim Hill, and Clarence Watson the moguls clearly perceived that modern mass industrialism had wrought profound changes in economic relations. For centuries craftsmen had grown, mined, or purchased raw materials which their labor turned into valuable items. When sold, the profit accrued to the craftsman. The workman lived by his skill and labor and earned, in the medieval expression, his livelihood. Industrialization shattered that system in an instant, together with all the cultural concepts that had grown out of it. Henceforth the capitalist would own the tools and control the sales; the worker would contribute raw labor in exchange for use of the tools. A contest for the profits arising from this new arrangement was certain to ensue. Since one side could decide where the profits would go, the owners quite naturally determined to seize them for themselves, leaving the workers a mere "living." To do this they had to act in unity, through associations of their common interests. Conversely, the laborers had to be denied the opportunity to act in unity. United action could spell victory; disunity could bring only defeat. Hence the universal opposition to labor unions throughout American indus-

try prior to the New Deal. In the primitive setting of the
Appalachian mineral fields, the contest erupted in bloody war-
fare which both sides recognized as such.

The "mine wars" in Appalachia were pushed with a fervor
and opposed with a determination never experienced elsewhere
in American society. The drabness of the mining camps and the
low wages of the coal fields during bleak and frequent depres-
sions made the miners and their wives desperate. Sometimes for
long intervals food consisted of coffee, cornbread, salt bacon,
and gravy made with pork grease, salt, white flour, and water.
The miners were without security in their homes because the
moguls reserved the right to terminate "the master-servant rela-
tionship" at will, evicting the occupants. In any given situation
the company owned or controlled as operating lessee all the
land and houses for miles around. Since the hapless miner could
find no other shelter, he could either accept the company's terms
of employment or he could get out and camp by a roadside.
Coal was the only industry, and the operators maintained black
lists of "ungrateful and uncooperative" miners. To be evicted for
union activities was to lose shelter, wages, and employment.
The miner—a foreign-born immigrant, a poor laborer from the
southern cotton fields or the Tennessee Valley, a black man up
from Mississippi or Alabama plantation serfdom, or a hillbilly
who had moved into the camp from a worn-out hillside farm—
had no savings, scant education, and no other salable skills. His
only hope lay in unity—in union—and it required incredible
bravery for him to grasp that slender reed. Efforts to organize
were invariably met with brutal repression and anti-organizing
injunctions, and frequently with death.[1]

This cycle produced spectacular rebellions. Irish miners calling themselves "The Sons of Molly Maguire" waged a guerrilla
war on the industry in western Pennsylvania in the 1870's, for
which no fewer than twenty were convicted and hanged.[2] The
Homestead massacre in the same state in 1892 involved a pitched
battle between miners and steelworkers on one side and a considerable legion of Pinkerton detectives on the other. The workers won that battle by shelling the Pinkertons with a cannon left
over from the Civil War, but in the end Andrew Carnegie and
Henry Clay Frick won the war.[3]

In the 1880's a devastating industrial war was fought in northern West Virginia, and in the 1920's the "Logan County War" pitted an army of thousands of miners against four hundred deputy sheriffs and the National Guard. The "Battle of Blair Mountain" lasted for two days and was fought with rifles, pistols, machine guns, an anti-aircraft gun, and a bomber. The "Matewan Massacre" rubbed out the mayor of the town, two miners, and seven Baldwin-Felts mine guards.[4]

In Harlan County, Kentucky, in the 1930's at least thirteen and probably twenty men died of gunshot wounds in a prolonged struggle to unionize. The persistence of the men and of the United Mine Workers of America was repeatedly thwarted until federal lawsuits and indictments demoralized the operators and forced the companies to sign a contract.[5] The drama of the bitter contest moved people to commemorate it in song and legend. A miner named Jim Garland composed "The Death of Harry Simms," which tells of the murder of a young volunteer organizer for the National Miners Union and is surely one of the most impressive of all American folksongs. His sister, Aunt Molly Jackson, wrote the moving "Poor Miner's Farewell," Sarah Gunning belted out "I Hate the Capitalist System." It was powerful propaganda during the hungry and desolate days of the 1930's:

> I hate the capitalist system,
> And I'll tell you the reason why:
> It has caused me endless suffering,
> And caused my friends to die.
>
> While the rich and mighty capitalist
> Goes dressed in jewels and silk,
> My darling blue-eyed baby
> Has died for the want of milk.

From Aunt Molly Jackson came another memorable refrain:

> I am a Union woman,
> As brave as I can be,
> And I don't like the bosses,
> And the bosses don't like me![6]

Out of this prolonged rebellion, repression, and bloodshed came a popular image of gallant miners on one side and cold-hearted, greedy, murderous mine barons on the other. In general this concept is valid, but it is a bit too simple. Starving and ragged people are always entitled to justice, and there has been little of that commodity in the coal fields. But the down side of the economic cycle—the bust—always caught workers and management alike. Companies that paid high wages during booms, because that was the only means by which workmen could be retained, were forced to pay less when the market was glutted and prices plunged. Invariably the bust produced unneeded miners, in a multitude that swelled as new technologies were introduced to eliminate them and their attendant wages (and, after 1937, their social security and unemployment insurance contributions). The misery and disillusionment produced by this mass unemployment sharpened the hatred of the workmen and their families and focused public hostility on the "heartless" operators.

The operators were indeed remarkably callous and ruthless. They did not hesitate to resort to bullet and bomb to "protect their property," and they willingly paid out millions to guards (or, as miners would say, "thugs") who would force destitute men to shovel coal all day for a wage barely sufficient to buy beans and cornbread for their children. Incomprehensibly, the operators sought no ways out of these dilemmas. They insisted that their only duty was to produce coal and that miners should work on their terms or move on. They held to the near-feudal notion that the mines, tipples, and houses were theirs to do with absolutely as they pleased, and that their duties to their workmen ended at the pay window. In an increasingly complex society this was not enough, and government had to pay from the public purse the costs wrought by such witless greed.

Some mine operators were scarcely literate self-made men who had struggled up from the coal pits or from cove farms. They scorned the miners and anyone else who threatened their "rights." Others had begun life as small merchants or county-seat lawyers and parlayed tiny nest eggs, hard work, resourcefulness, and luck into underfinanced shack villages, ramshackle commissaries with barren offices upstairs, tipples, and a few mine headings. They provided no schoolhouses, leaving that function entirely to the counties. Their "sanitary facilities" were tottering, filthy privies. Their streets were stretches of mud and cinders. They built no hospitals and never considered the possibility of a library. Such cultural primitives could be expected to have scant sympathy for a workman or for anyone else. Their entire objective was to make money. Some of them accumulated wealth on a modest scale, but they scarcely deserved to be called moguls.[7]

Much more representative of the coal operators as a class were men of good education, impeccable manners, and long familiarity with the good life. They did not incur the hatred of their workers and the obloquy of succeeding generations simply because they lacked education or because some other "disadvantages" had befallen them. If the world in which they built their towns and operated their mines was an imperfect one, it was nevertheless conceived by them and by others of their genre. They made their own world, and they should have made it better. To their discredit, it must be noted that they consistently withheld their vaunted philanthropies from the miners. Their charities were in the cities where they lived, never in the villages from which they derived their wealth.

A look at a few of these "rich and mighty capitalists" will suffice to illustrate the diversity and, simultaneously, the similarity of their backgrounds. Studying their faces in old photographs, pondering their degrees and accomplishments, and considering the corporate paternalism they uniformly espoused in the early days, one finds it hard to escape the conclusion that they were basically men of good will. They wanted to make money, to build broad halls to wander through, to enjoy long, gleaming motorcars driven by liveried chauffeurs, and to partake of the good life on occasional trips to Paris, London, and Rome. Most of them liked to read, possessed libraries, and could discourse learnedly on public issues. They preferred to see families well fed, well educated, and content.[8]

But their world was full of contradictions. They hated to pay taxes because taxes reduced their profits. By holding taxes to insanely low levels, they guaranteed poor schools for the children of their miners, insuring that the region would henceforth be blighted by widespread illiteracy, ignorance, and poverty.[9] The moguls preferred to pay adequate wages, but in times of depression an adequate wage meant coal unsold, or sold at a loss. So they imposed low wages, and balladeers sang of babies "dead for the want of milk." The situation became an economic and social quagmire from which there was no escape under laissez-faire principles and practices.[10]

Then these men of basically decent instincts were hit by a world event that drove them quite literally mad. In 1917 revolution broke out in czarist Russia. Peasants, laborers, and soldiers who had endured all that flesh could bear tore the old order apart. The revolution passed into the hands of Lenin and his followers, and "liquidations" ensued. Property was confiscated from "the capitalists"; ownership passed to "the people." Once-wealthy industrialists fled in rags to the West. "Workers of the World Unite!" became the Bolshevik slogan, and a worldwide revolution of "workers" against "capitalists" was proclaimed at Communist party conferences. In America there were Communists—not many of them, but enough to demonstrate that Marxism had its adherents. The National Miners Union was Red-sponsored and in the early 1930's appeared in the coal fields. The vast structure of capitalism—banks, insurance companies, industry, all the comforts and prerogatives of money—suddenly felt itself besieged. The Communists were out there. They were coming to "stir up trouble." The foundations of "Americanism" were in danger. To the moguls it appeared very clear: the enlightened and educated were under assault by the ignorant and greedy, the Christians were besieged by the godless. Stage by stage they convinced themselves that their danger was real and immediate and that it must be confronted and thwarted. Since they were "right" and their adversaries were "wrong," any weapon was deemed justifiable. Persuasion and cajolery were best, but if they failed, machine guns were not out of the question. Fight fire with fire! Stop at nothing! Win or die!

The enemy was not the Red dictator in Moscow, who probably did not know that the coal camps and towns of eastern Kentucky existed. Rather, the adversary was in those camps, consisting of the miners and their gaunt wives and, invariably, those "outsiders" who sympathized with them. The outsiders were journalists, labor organizers, liberal politicians, students, or anyone else who chanced to pass through or who wrote an article critical of management or supportive of workers. Paranoia crept into the valleys like a choking gray smog, lethal and unreasoning. It poisoned all relationships, deepened chasms between the classes, ruled out almost any consideration of reform, and paralyzed the owners into inaction. In their fright the owners rejected the idea of providing leadership in solving the social and economic problems that besieged them on every front.

On March 23, 1928, Richard B. Mellon, former chairman of the board of the giant Pittsburgh Coal Company, appeared as a witness before the Senate committee on interstate commerce. He testified that he owned 11 percent of the corporation's stock. He was asked by Senator Burton Wheeler whether he had visited the company's mine villages to look at the conditions "under which those employees of yours and their families are living." He replied, "I have not been out there; no." Pittsburgh Coal was then operating with non-union labor and had long been convulsed by strikes. The miners claimed that their families could not be supported on the wage scale that the company had unilaterally posted. The board had turned deaf ears to their pleas for higher wages and then had appropriated $15,000 for support of a missionary to save their souls.

Mellon, demonstrating a total blindness to these incongruities, saw nothing wrong with setting up machine guns in the coal towns to coerce their populations: "It is necessary. You could not run without them."[11] His attitudes were typical of the kings of coal, coke, and steel. In her magnificent "Come Join the C.I.O.," Aunt Molly Jackson summed up the madness of such gentlemen:

> I was raised in old Kentucky
> In Kentucky borned and bred,
> But when I joined the Union
> They called me a Rooshian Red.

Charles Edward Hellier was one Kentucky gentleman who harbored such attitudes. He associated with other gentlemen, gave them legal advice, and was charmed by their handsome wives. As a good Republican he believed in stability and perceived, quite naturally, that money and power gravitated to the hands of those best qualified to use them. The lower orders deserved a fair share, of course; but gentlemen of education and background could be expected to see to their needs.

Hellier was born in Bangor, Maine, in 1864. His Puritan ancestors came over in 1630 aboard the *Arbella* with Governor William Bradford. His forebears fought in the nation's wars from the earliest times; one, his great-grandfather, was with Benedict Arnold during his campaign against Quebec. His father, Walter, was a merchant and farmer "distinguished alike for his firm integrity of character, devotion to his family, and application to business." (In other words, he loved both God and Mammon.) As a boy Charles loved to read the English classics and the biographies of notable people. He attended high school at Bangor, graduated from Yale in 1886, did postgraduate work at the University of Berlin, and then obtained a law degree at Boston University. He practiced law at Boston and numbered among his friends and clients such genteel souls as James Murray Forbes and Warren Delano, the Forbes supercargo, and Delano's son of the same name.

The younger Delano interested Hellier in the eastern Kentucky coal fields, then up for grabs in county-size spreads and at ridiculously low prices. A syndicate called the Elk Horn Coal & Coke Company was formed to buy up lands in the valley of the Big Sandy River, and the tireless Delano crossed over the hills from Harlan and his labors with Kentenia to arrange purchases. They acquired about 70,000 acres in "the famous Elk Horn coal fields, probably the most valuable in the world." In 1902 the syndicate changed their name to the Big Sandy Company, of which Hellier was elected president. He and his friends among the Boston moguls persuaded the C&O to build a hundred miles of track from the old terminus at Whitehouse to Ash Camp on Marrow Bone Creek in Pike County. In that "hitherto isolated district rich both in timber and mineral resources" they built Hellier, Kentucky, another town conceived as a model of good housing and corporate paternalism. Its twin tipples processed many millions of tons of Kentucky's finest coal in the next half-century. Hellier organized or served as director of a dozen additional companies during the ensuing years and "was ever alive to the duties of citizenship." He was a devoted member of the

Natural History Society of Massachusetts, the Massachusetts Horticultural Society, the University Club of New York, the University and Engineers Club of Boston, the Graduates Club of New Haven, and the Beverly Yacht Club. He married Mary Harman of New Haven, Connecticut, in 1886 and they had four children.

Hellier was neat and debonair, with a crisply trimmed mustache. His expensive tweeds, conservative colors, immaculate white shirts and starched collars blended harmoniously with his college degrees, Episcopalian worship, and discreet bookishness. He was the antithesis of redneck and hillbilly—a true New England blueblood who had the prudence to acquire a secure position in Kentucky coal.[12]

Augustus Foscoe Whitfield was born in the Alabama town of Demopolis on Christmas Day, 1861. He, too, descended from old colonial stock, and his face was as strong and craggy as an Appalachian cliff. His first American forebear, Matthew Whitfield, used his own ship to bring indentured colonists to Virginia in the 1670's. Augustus Whitfield attended private schools, then studied for two years at the Alabama Polytechnic Institute. He joined the Army Signal Corps and in 1887 was sent to Arizona as director of the U.S. Weather Bureau. He campaigned against Geronimo in one of the last Indian wars. Leaving the service, he worked for a time as a railroad surveyor, and in 1891 he turned his talents to buying up mineral lands in northern Alabama for various coal companies. In 1899 he organized his own firms, the Black Creek Coal Company and the Warrior Pratt Coal Company near Porter, Alabama. With several thousand acres of Alabama minerals secured, he and his brother Bryan turned to the treasures available in Harlan County. In 1911 they sold out their southern holdings and invested in the Clover Fork Coal Company at Kitts, and in Harlan Collieries at Brookside. They built the usual array of houses, tipples, and stores and recruited workers to occupy them. In 1919 the brothers divided the properties, with Augustus retaining the works at Kitts.

Whitfield was a director of several coal-related companies in the Harlan-Middlesboro area. He was a friend of John C. C. Mayo and C. Bascom Slemp, and he acquired 3,000 shares in

Kentucky River Coal Corporation. A staunch advocate of soil conservation, he wrote learned articles on the subject which were published in *Agricultural Engineering*. He was a member of the American Society of Agricultural Engineers, a thirty-second degree Mason, and senior warden of Christ Episcopal Church at Harlan. He was a political rarity, a staunch Republican from the Deep South. He detested the New Deal with its "Red leanings" and, as a leading member of the Harlan County Coal Operators' Association, strove prodigiously to rout communism and unionism. At his funeral, in 1947, the old Indian fighter wore the white apron of a Master Mason.[13]

Howard N. Eavenson was a friend and beleaguered ally of the Whitfield brothers. His photograph suggests an intense man, agitated and ill at ease. He was a Quaker from Philadelphia who obtained his B.S. degree from Swarthmore in 1895. His first work as an engineer was with the Tennessee Coal & Iron Company. After a subsequent stint with Continental Coke Company at Uniontown, Pennsylvania, he moved to Lynch as chief engineer at that fantastic new operation. After 1920 he worked as a consulting engineer in several states until he decided to strike out on his own. In 1926 he organized the Clover Splint Coal Company in Harlan County. He struggled with the vexations of operating a mine and camp until 1947. He died six years later.

Eavenson, a highly respected member of his profession, may have had no peer as a mining engineer in America. He wrote learned books and articles on the history, methodology, and pitfalls of mining, including *The First Century and a Quarter of the American Coal Industry, Coal through the Ages*, and *The Pittsburgh Coal Bed—Its Early History and Development*. He was a member of the American Society of Mining and Metallurgical Engineers, the American Society of Civil Engineers, and the American Association for the Advancement of Science. That his interests were broader and deeper than those of his colleagues is demonstrated by his membership in the American Academy of Political and Social Sciences and in the American Economic Society. Eavenson received an honorary degree from the University of Pittsburgh in 1928, the Perry Nichols Medal in 1947, and the Lawrence Saunders Gold Medal of the American Institute of Mining in 1950. He was a member of Tau Beta Pi,

Delta Epsilon, and the University and Duquesne Clubs of Pittsburgh. He was also a devoted traveler and tennis player.

A moderating influence in the usually immoderate councils of the Harlan County Coal Operators' Association, Eavenson was deeply troubled by the turmoils that swept the coal fields and his own mines. He deserved to live in a less tumultuous time and place.[14]

Robert Lyon Stearns, a co-founder of Stearns Coal & Lumber Company, was another Yankee who traced his ancestry to a Puritan immigrant. He had extensive lumber operations in the white pine country of Michigan, and when that noble tree grew scarce he moved to McCreary County, Kentucky, to combine lumbering and coal mining. He acquired for his company 107,000 acres in Kentucky and Tennessee. His sawmill, the largest in Kentucky, was the first electric one. In 1904 Stearns Coal & Lumber built the Kentucky & Tennessee Railroad to gain a connection with the Southern Railway.

In the first decade of the twentieth century he and his father, Justus Stearns, opened the Justus Mine and built the town of Stearns, providing it with electric lights, running water, a sewerage system, a recreation building, and telephones. His mines produced Blue Heron coal and his sawmills turned out a comprehensive line of hard and soft wood products. In World War I he was chairman of the McCreary County draft board and obtained so many volunteers that the federal government named a Liberty ship the *McCreary*.

But Stearns hated labor unions, and he maintained a tight blacklist. On Christmas Day, 1908, three labor organizers working in his town defied an order to leave, and a United States marshal and two local lawmen died in the ensuing gun battle. When the organizers holed up in the Stearns Hotel, the tycoon promptly ordered his building torched so they could be shot as they fled the flames.

He sat on the boards of several corporations in Kentucky and Michigan and is remembered as a man of "unfailing fairness." Stearns did not devote all his time to business, however, but wrote a series of books which have been called "witty" and "charming": *The Lumberman's Primer*, *The Ass and the Barnacles*, *Ossawald Crum*, and *Had Marco Polo Travelled West In-*

stead of East. This relaxed, jaunty, and humorous man died in 1939 at the age of sixty-seven, in the bosom of the Congregationalist church and the Republican party.[15]

George C. Westervelt married a daughter of Daniel Langhorne of Lynchburg, Virginia. His wife, Rieta, inherited substantial stock holdings in Kentucky River Coal (of which her father was a founder), and the Langhorne group put him on the board in 1933. He served as chairman for fourteen years before his death in 1956. The Langhornes could not have found a more seasoned businessman to protect their tribal interest.

Westervelt was of Dutch stock. His ancestors came to America in about 1662. Born in Texas, he was educated at Corpus Christi and at the United States Naval Academy. He received an M.S. degree from the Massachusetts Institute of Technology in 1907. While he was in the navy Westervelt met William E. Boeing, a Seattle furnituremaker; the two men were aviation enthusiasts and combined their financial, technical, and managerial resources to form the Boeing Aircraft Corporation. Westervelt designed the company's first airplane in 1915, and it was built at Boeing's furniture factory. During World War I he was in charge of all aircraft procurement for the navy, and he was senior naval member of the joint Army-Navy Aeronautical Commission. After the war he directed the construction of the navy's giant dirigible, the Z-2. Upon leaving the navy in 1922, he became vice-president of the Glenn Davis Properties, Inc., and was later associated with North American Aviation, Inc. In subsequent years he climbed through practically the entire evolving U.S. aircraft industry, holding positions in Sperry Gyroscope, Curtiss-Wright, Ford Instrument, Intercontinental Aviation, and China National Aviation.

The stage also intrigued Westervelt, who wrote twenty-seven plays, four of which were produced on Broadway: *Romancing 'Round* (1926), *The Iron General* (formerly entitled *Mongolia*; 1927), *The Blimp* (1929), and *Down to Miami* (1944).

After another retirement in the early 1930's, Westervelt acquired a 40,000-acre cattle ranch, dealt in Florida real estate, and worked as an engineering consultant. In World War II he oversaw the construction in Bombay of a gigantic floating drydock for Great Britain. In both engineering and business acumen he was one of the foremost men of his time.[16]

In the 1920's the immensely rich (and equally brutal and corrupt) Mellon family and their banks and trust company put together a utility holding company to supply gas, coal, and other fuels to New York and Massachusetts. Called Eastern Gas & Fuel Associates, it derived much of its income from the sale of gas and chemicals from the enormously productive coke ovens of its sister company, Koppers. The heirs of old Thomas Mellon, judge, banker, and land broker, had quietly assembled the greatest fortune in the United States. Their companies also included Aluminum Company of America, Carborundum Corporation, Pittsburgh Glass, Pittsburgh Coal, Union Steel, Mellon National Bank, and Gulf Oil. The head of the clan was Andrew, a billionaire by 1930 and austere chief of the "Mellon ring" whose money and coercive use (or denial) of jobs, credit, and philanthropies dominated the Keystone State for two decades.

In 1930 Koppers Coal acquired Weeksbury and vast acreages of toluol-rich by-product coal in Floyd County. German chemists had wrested a long catalogue of derivatives from the gases that Henry Clay Frick had routinely expelled into the Pennsylvania countryside. Mellon grants to the University of Pittsburgh added many more substances to the list. The coal dug by the miners at Weeksbury appeared in paints, dyes, medicines, fabrics, explosives, wood preservatives, tar, and furnace gas. Eventually title went over to Eastern Gas & Fuel Associates, but the hands at the helm were always those of Mellons.

The Mellon-owned Pittsburg Coal built a modern community of about 250 houses and gave it the lovely name of Betsey Layne, for a pioneer woman whose descendants peopled the area.

The Mellon fortune was built on cheap labor, monopoly of raw materials and patents, exploding demand brought on by wars and economic booms, and effective control over the government's power to put down rebellions in the hideous steel, coal, and coke towns of Appalachia and the oil fields of Latin America. State police and the U.S. Marines were always available to the Mellons.

After Warren Harding's inauguration, Andrew Mellon became known as "the secretary." He ruled the Treasury Department for eleven years and persuaded Congress to adopt the "Mellon plan" of large tax cuts for people with large incomes. He said the cuts would stimulate expansion of the nation's industrial plant and assure prolonged prosperity. They stimulated speculation, too, and a wild stock market binge that ended in the 1929 crash. In 1932 Herbert Hoover shipped "the greatest Secretary of the Treasury since Alexander Hamilton" off to London as ambassador to the Court of St. James. As he departed, newspaper scribes wrote (only partly in jest) that "three presidents had served under Andrew W. Mellon."

As a mogul, only the first Rockefeller could compare with the icy banker. Sometimes in the oilfields the armies of the two tycoons fought each other with dynamite and rifles. The "Mellon crowd" and the "Standard crowd" were amazingly similar in ethnic backgrounds, cultural roots, religious preferences, and relentless greediness. However, the Standard money eventually concentrated in New York, while the Mellon machine stayed rooted in Pittsburgh, the industrial capital of Appalachia.

The Mellon holdings in eastern Kentucky appeared huge when seen from the perspective of the little state capital of Frankfort. Viewed from the Mellon suites at Pittsburgh, however, they were small parts of a global empire. When the best of the coal was gone, the towns, their people, and the depleted coal veins were dropped as pitilessly as if they had been cinders from a steel mill.[17]

J. Gardner Bradley, who ran mines across the Big Sandy in West Virginia, was the quintessence of the upper-class industrialist who knew what was best for his miners and was determined to see that they got it, even if it killed them. He was born in New Jersey in 1881 and graduated from Harvard Law School in 1904. Bradley inherited huge land holdings from his mother, who had inherited them in turn from her father, Simon Cameron. Cameron twice served in the Senate from Pennsylvania, plus a short stint as Lincoln's secretary of war. He was notoriously corrupt, and his service as commissioner of Winnebago Indian claims resulted in a national scandal: some of the vanished appropriations that Congress had intended for the Winnebagos may have gone into the extensive coal lands he acquired in West Virginia.

Bradley spent his life building railroads into the Gauley and Elk River regions of the state and organizing and managing coal corporations. He sat on the boards of eleven corporations and family trusts and was a member of seven social clubs, including the ultra-prestigious Harvard Club of New York City. He was one of the West Virginia Constitutional and Library Commissioners, chairman of the West Virginia YMCA committee, and a trustee of the Boston Library Society. His professional memberships included the National Coal Association (of which he became president in 1921), West Virginia Coal Association, American Mining Congress (of which he was president during 1927–28, the American Institute of Mining, Metallurgical and Petroleum Engineers, the Southern States Industrial Council, and the Pennsylvania and West Virginia Bar Associations. He was a prominent Republican and a delegate to the party's national conventions in 1916 and 1928.

Bradley waged a vicious campaign against his employees when they sought to unite for their common economic welfare. He organized gangs of armed goons, imported machine guns, obtained court injunctions against men who engaged in "criminal syndicalism" by joining the United Mine Workers, and finally crushed their effort. One published biographical sketch describes his philanthropic achievement as follows: "Bradley considered that his chief contribution to the welfare of his employees was his successful thwarting of efforts by the United Mine Workers of America to unionize them. In the 1940's, because of his resistance to unionization, the Elk River Company was involved in one of the longest strikes in the history of West Virginia and state police had to protect company grounds frequently."[18]

Bradley claimed that the principles by which he lived were the doctrines of the Episcopal church and the Constitution of the United States as it was interpreted by the Supreme Court prior to 1933. He died in Boston in 1971.

Fortunately, not every Bradley was so draconian. Perhaps William Aspinwall Bradley imbibed some of the social notions of his cousin Franklin Delano Roosevelt. A New York banker, he vacationed in the Kentucky hills for several summers between 1900 and 1930 and became a careful and generally sympathetic observer of the hill people. He published a number of articles about the locals and their culture; they were pieces of a kind then much in vogue, but they indicate that at least one mogul saw something in eastern Kentucky other than mines and profits. While his "visits" were doubtless inspection trips, too, with keen observation of how funds were being invested, Bradley did not fail to see that industrialization was shattering a culture. His articles appeared in *Harper's*, *The Dial*, and *Scribner's* in 1915 and 1918 and should be read by anyone interested in now largely vanished Appalachian folkways.[19]

In 1917 Bradley published a slender volume of poetry entitled *Old Christmas and Other Kentucky Tales in Verse*. Critics may question the value of his work, but there is a haunting quality about his poems. One of them, "Men of Harlan," was inspired by the sight of a long file of mountaineers making their way along Lexington's main street:

> Here in the level country,
>   Where the streets run straight and wide,
> Six men upon their pacing nags
>   May travel side by side,
> But the mountain men of Harlan,
>   You may tell them all the while,
> When they pass through our village,
>   For they ride in single file.
> And the children when they see them,
>   Stop their play and stand and cry:
> "Here come the men of Harlan,
>   Men of Harlan, riding by."
>
> O, the mountain men of Harlan,
>   When they come down to the plain,
> With dangling stirrup, jangling spur,
>   and loosely hanging rein,
> They do not ride like our folks here,
>   In twos and threes abreast,
> With merry laughter, talk and song
>   And lightly spoken jest.
> But silently and solemnly,
>   In long and straggling line,
> As you may see them in the hills,
>   Beyond Big Black and Pine.
>
> For in that far, strange country,
>   Where the men of Harlan dwell,

There are no roads at all like ours,
  As we've heard travelers tell.
But only narrow trails that wind
  Along each shallow creek,
Where the silence hangs so heavy,
  You can hear the leathers squeak.
And there no two can ride abreast,
  But each alone must go,
Picking his way as best he may
  With careful steps and slow.

Down many a shelving ledge of shale,
  Skirting the trembling sands,
Through many a pool and many a pass,
  Where the mountain laurel stands
So thick and close to left and right,
  With holly bushes, too,
The clinging branches meet midway
  To bar the passage through—
O'er many a steep and stony ridge,
  O'er many a high divide.
And so it is the Harlan men
  Thus one by one do ride.

Yet it is strange to see them pass
  in line through our wide street,
When they come down to sell their sang
  and buy their stores of meat,
These silent men, in somber black
  All clad from foot to head,
Though they have left their lonely hills,
  And the narrow creek's rough bed.
And 'tis no wonder children stop
  their play and stand and cry:
"Here come the men of Harlan,
  Men of Harlan, riding by."[20]

Then there was Godfrey Lowell Cabot, of the Boston Cabots (who, according to a venerable toast, are so lofty that they "speak only to God"). He owned 120,000 acres of West Virginia land and spoke quite heatedly to his fellow moguls in their association meetings whenever a bunch of ungrateful miners asked for higher wages.

Hellier, Whitfield, Eavenson, Stearns, Westervelt, and the Bradleys—these men typify the masters of coal in the Age of the Moguls. In Kentucky, West Virginia, Tennessee, and Virginia the pattern of ownership was the same: numerous locally spawned semiliterate operators of small mines, and a dominant crowd of mostly northern tycoons with degrees from the best universities and memberships in the most exclusive clubs.

Jim Garland's famous song about the murder of his young friend, Harry Simms, proclaims:

> Harry Simms was a pal of mine,
>   We labored side by side
> Expecting to be shot on sight,
>   Or taken for a ride,
> By them dirty operator gun thugs
>   That roamed from town to town,
> Shooting down poor union men
>   Where'er they could be found—

These men exemplify the "rich and mighty capitalists" who hired "them dirty operator gun thugs."

History must have a lesson for us in the relative manner in which the passing years have dealt with the coal operators and the balladeers who sang about them. Today the ballads of Jim Garland, Aunt Molly Jackson, and Sarah Gunning are still sold in record shops. The three appeared on campuses and in festivals to recall with music and song the bloody struggles of an earlier time. Their works have been collected and have an honored place in American folk music.

But who remembers the moguls?

NINE

After the Ball Was Over

SEVERAL YEARS AGO an old miner told me what it was like in eastern Kentucky between 1910 and 1920, the splendid decade of coal:

> Back then the operators had a ball. They built coal camps all over the place and took in money hand over fist. The biggest show in these mountains was their big special trains. They drove around in White Steamers and limousines that would make a Cadillac look tacky. They had the prettiest women in the country and, oh brother, how they did dress! If they wanted anything done they just called up the judge or governor or whoever had the power, and he got busy and took care of it for 'em. If they didn't like a body they told him to get out of the county, and he got out! They told ever'body how to vote, and if they didn't like a candidate he didn't have a chance. They lived sort of like a bunch of kings.[1]

In *The Robber Barons* Matthew Josephson describes America's moguls in their golden age, using words that fit eastern Kentucky's coal tycoons in their heyday:

> In short order the railroad presidents, the copper barons, the big dry goods merchants and the steel masters became Senators, ruling in the highest councils of the national government, and sometimes scattered twenty dollar gold pieces to newsboys of Washington. But they became, in even greater numbers, lay leaders of churches, trustees of universities, partners or owners of newspapers or news services and figures of fashionable, cultured society. And through all these channels they labored to advance their policies and principles, sometimes directly, more often with skillful indirection.[2]

As has been noted, two of the region's tycoons, Clarence Wayland Watson and Johnson Newlon Camden, Jr., became U.S. senators, while numerous others sat as state legislators and party bosses. For example, two members of the Harlan County Coal Operators' Association were chairmen of the local Republican and Democratic parties. Coal company lawyers and executives routinely served as members of county tax equalization boards, appellate panels that made sure the tax commissioners did not lay unfair burdens on taxpayers. In the incorporated company towns only company-approved candidates ran for municipal offices; in some of them no one ran at all, and the industrialists simply handed lists of desired officials to the county judges, who appointed them to "fill the vacancies." In many judicial districts the county and circuit court judges were coal operators or held stock in mining companies.

Company-paid policemen ruled the streets and sidewalks of more than two hundred mining towns and camps. Money prevailed in most elections, and the only people who had it to contribute in significant sums were the coal operators. In 1921 in Perry County alone there were 253 deputy sheriffs, and 26 men were shot to death within six weeks of the 1921 general election—all but four of them deputy sheriffs or the victims of deputy sheriffs.[3] The rule of coal, while not unchallenged, was complete.

Balls always end, and kings sometimes lose their crowns. The moguls thrived in those days when income and inheritance taxes were mere nuisances. Their excesses fueled a towering speculative boom that ended in 1929, and the rich were never so overtly powerful again. Much of their arrogance and the old flair with which they lived drained away with the collapse of their flamboyant age. The moguls who followed them forsook the limelight. Like Paul Mellon at his estate at Upperville, Virginia, they sought seclusion and left management to a class of rising professionals. Although the iron fist of wealth did not lose its grip, it did put on a velvet glove.

After John D. Rockefeller's daughter Edith married Harold McCormick, an heir to the huge International Harvester fortune, her happy father bought $30 million worth of Harvester stock.[4] Thus Harlan County's two giants, at Benham and Lynch, lay in Pendragon's clutches. When he backed the great merger of the West Virginia, Pennsylvania, and Maryland companies into Consolidation Coal in 1909, he became a substantial investor in its stock. Then, in 1915, he bought most of the corporation's bonded indebtedness. (In 1928 his son told a congressional committee that he held 28 percent of its common and 72 percent of its preferred shares.[5]) Thus the prince of moguls dominated eastern Kentucky's three largest mining operations. He kept his grip during the boom years just before and during World War I and, according to men who worked in the company offices at that time, his son visited Jenkins on "inspection tours" at least twice in the 1920's. When or whether Pendragon sold his stock is unknown, but the fate of the lesser moguls who industrialized the region is much clearer.

The circumstances that shattered the grand hopes and pleasant world of the coal moguls deserve examination. The tycoons were crushed by forces of their own making, the deadliest of all a force that lay within them: greed.

In the beginning of the era of Appalachia's industrialization, the nation's energy base was shifting from the water power of New England to steam and coal. As the shift continued, the demand for coal expanded mightily; it was used to heat houses and factories, to energize mills and power plants, and to propel ships and locomotives. As the expansion continued, an optimism bordering on euphoria arose in coal circles. The magnates opened mines in Pennsylvania and Maryland, then marched westward, gobbling up extensive new fields in West Virginia, Virginia, Tennessee, Kentucky, and Alabama. Between 1890 and 1920 annual coal production in the United States rose from 156 million to 597 million tons.

But even in the 1880's there were severe problems. So many people had left the monotonous backcountry farms and so many trainloads of immigrants had joined them that there were often labor gluts. Because not even the tedious methods of mining then employed could use all those hands, there were strikes and "wars" in all the states. Relationships between master and man grew embittered, and still are.[6]

New technologies grew up to displace steam. Electricity began to shoulder out steam plants, and Rudolph Diesel's invention opened a new area of competition, as diesels replaced coal on ships and in many factories. The oil age flourished with the discovery of one new petroleum field after another.

Munitions industries used much coal during World War I, and for a couple of years thereafter the European mines were in disarray. Then the French, English, and German pits got underway again and the export market dissolved. Simultaneously the shipbuilders shifted to fuel oil. Scientists devised improved ways of burning coal so that more heat could be extracted from it. The power companies built hydro-electric plants. Texas petroleum became almost as cheap as water. Suddenly, around 1921, it began to dawn upon rich and powerful men that there simply were not enough markets to keep eastern Kentucky's gigantic new industry always at work. Between 1920 and 1922 American coal output plummeted by 164 million tons, and the number of men employed in America's soft coal mines fell by 200,000.[7] During the previous decade the population of the mining region had more than doubled; indeed, in the Poor Fork area of Harlan County it had risen an incredible 900 percent. Eastern Kentucky coal production soared from 8,617,193 tons in 1912 to 24,492,504 tons in 1920. The tens of thousands of people who had abandoned farms and left homes in distant countries to take up the miner's tools had cast their lot with the moguls and had effectively burned their economic bridges. For most there was no going back to the old order. They had left an ancient familistic society for the coal camp and the paternalism of the big bosses. This shift from reliance on kin (familism) to reliance on company (paternalism) was of historic importance to the Appalachian people. Having previously looked to settled, traditional family-oriented society for guidance and stability, they now had to look to the benevolence of Howard N. Eavenson, Robert Lyon Stearns, Augustus Foscue Whitfield, Charles E. Hellier, George C. Westervelt, the Watsons, Flemings, and Haymonds of the Fairmont ring, the Mellons of Pittsburgh, the members of the Rockefeller–Standard Oil combine, and the other owners of eastern Kentucky's multitudinous coal camps and towns. The "hands" expected the coal men to keep the system working and those indispensable payroll and scrip windows open. Not only had the moguls caused an economic upheaval in the hills; they had simultaneously brought about a profound cultural and social revolution. Neither the miners nor the moguls understood or were prepared for its consequences.[8]

In the early 1920's catastrophe befell much of the industry. Confronting a shrunken market with a flood of production, there was no escape for those scores of small companies with their rows of barren shacks and swarms of men blasting inferior coal from thin seams. Elk Horn Coal, Consolidation Coal, and the bigger and more efficient operations in the thick seams of Harlan County staggered but survived. Their heat-rich coal absorbed the market while the lesser firms shut down. When new orders failed to come, the scrip windows in these poorly capitalized operations were slammed shut and the commissary doors were locked. Malcolm Ross's *Machine Age in the Hills* describes in graphic terms the social chaos of those dead towns in the 1920's. In an age without public welfare programs, the miners were sustained by occasional days of employment—days made possible only because they agreed to work for trifles. Towns that carried such names as Ice (for another operator from Fairmont), Dalna, Bellecraft, Red Star, Bastin, Woodrock, Happy, Parsons, Edgewater, Carbon Glow, Bluefield, Kay-Jay, Elsiecoal, and Mayking began their gradual disappearance from the earth. The departure of these weak companies from the market marked the advent of a calamitous labor depression that would not abate for twenty years. Across America coal employment eroded at the staggering rate of nearly 1,700 per month for ten grim years. The hills swarmed with miners who could find no work; for scores of companies there was no escape from bankruptcy. One not wholly atypical operator turned down an offer of $750,000 for his investment, then saw the sheriff sell it a few years later for $4,000, his tipple and machines going to a junk dealer.[9]

Amid the economic and social wreckage of the 1920's, the big towns—the Watson communities and others of comparable quality—survived as enclaves of relative prosperity. They captured the coal orders for two reasons: they had the best coal and the necessary connections. Despite the collapse of untold numbers of small independent operations, the mines of the moguls produced even more, prospering amid deepening general ruin.

By 1929 coal production had inched up to 542 million tons—a respectable figure, but still substantially below that of 1917.

For Consol, Elk Horn Coal, and the Fairmont ring, the real trouble began with the stock market crash. George W. Fleming had gone off to New York to wheel and deal. In the euphoria of ever-rising prices only an iron-willed man could fail to speculate, and only a genius could get out in time. Clarence Wayland Watson, James Otis Watson II, and Fleming speculated heavily. They not only spent their own money on vastly overpriced stocks but also invested money borrowed from the National Bank of Fairmont, which they controlled.[10] Their losses were appalling—in the case of Clarence Wayland Watson, probably at least $16 million. A dozen millionaires in the Monongahela Valley around Fairmont were left destitute.[11]

Watson encountered severe difficulties before the 1929 crash wiped out most of his wealth. After 1913, senators were chosen in popular elections rather than by the corrupt state legislatures. In an attempt to gain a full term in 1918, Watson, who was then chairman of Consol's board, approached the officials of the United Mine Workers with a proposition. He told John L. Lewis that the strongly anti-union Consolidation would sign a contract with the union if the miners would vote for him. A secret compact was made and Consol signed the labor agreement, thereby compelling other companies in West Virginia's northern field to do likewise. Although the miners kept their end of the bargain and voted almost solidly for him, his "Wilson Wants Watson" reelection campaign failed. Another coal tycoon was elected, leaving Watson with that burdensome contract—and with the wrath of the coal industry as well. In 1924 he unilaterally renounced this "Baltimore agreement"; lesser companies followed suit, and the entire field was racked with strikes and a prolonged and bloody labor war. Although this debacle cost Watson the respect of other operators and brought him the undying hatred of the miners, in 1927 he boasted that he had completely purged the Consol's operations of all involvement with labor unions.[12]

Consol's pre-Depression production peaked in 1927 at 12,768,704 tons, a million more than in 1917, but the stock market crash and ensuing deflation overwhelmed the company.

In 1928 the Rockefeller interests had reorganized Consol's management and dropped Watson. On June 2, 1932, a federal court in Maryland appointed receivers for the once high-flying combine.[13] In due time Elk Horn Coal followed suit. The Fairmont ring lay in ruins—bereft of political office, its companies under court supervision and a mere hair's breadth from bankruptcy. The National Bank of Fairmont closed with a loss of millions to its depositors and shareholders. Investors who had bought shares in their mining companies blamed the Watsons and Flemings, and especially the fallen senator, for their losses. The battered "king of coal" was in such disfavor with his fellow townsmen that he was compelled to remain secluded at his Fairmont home, creeping in and out under cover of darkness.

In its effort to stay afloat, Elk Horn sold off many of its properties. The gas and oil rights went for $1 million—only a trifle more than $4 per acre. As previously noted, the town of Weeksbury and many thousands of acres had already been bought by the canny Mellons of Pittsburgh. Another huge territory and the town of Wheelwright passed to Inland Steel. When the selling ended, about 134,000 acres and four towns remained.

The senator and his baronial colleagues tried to adapt to a changed way of life. Gone forever were the resplendent private railroad cars and chartered trains, the trips to Europe on stately liners, the liveried chauffeurs and gleaming limousines. James Otis Watson II wangled a federal job from his old friend Franklin Roosevelt. The aged and frustrated Clarence Wayland Watson died in 1940, powerless and all but forgotten.[14]

The decline of the moguls can be traced in the fate of their mansions. The Fleming house became headquarters for the Fairmont Woman's Club. James Otis Watson's magnificent Highgate was turned into a funeral home; solemn mourners now gather in its once-festive halls. The senator's stately LaGrange became an ill-kept apartment house. The manicured farm which the "father of the West Virginia coal industry" bequeathed to his children and where Clarence Wayland Watson kept his splendid thoroughbreds was divided into lots and mini-farms.[15]

At Paintsville, Alice Mayo abandoned the proud hall John C. C. had built for her and, with the aid of a new husband, erected a somewhat less pretentious new mansion down the Big Sandy at Ashland. Mayo's mighty house stood empty for a while then was sold for use as a school. Its rooms were subdivided into dingy cubicles, the rich paneling assumed a gloomy darkness, and the vaunted allegorical paintings vanished—probably beneath coats of bland wall paint.[16] Even the new mansion suffered degradation, sheltering boarders for a time during the depths of the Depression. Eventually it followed the example of its predecessor and went on the auction block. Today it houses a medical clinic, and only a few local residents recall that it was once owned by a family named Mayo.

Haymond Hall at West Virginia Wesleyan College in Buckhannon and the Fleming Memorial Church in Fairmont survive as muted monuments to the grandeur of two other fallen tycoons.

After the fall of the Fairmont ring, new men fashioned fresh policies for humbled corporations. They bowed to the New Deal's labor laws and made peace with the workers. Where moguls once had imperiously fought unionists, compromisers made a tenuous peace. From 1933 to 1959 practically every operation in the valleys of the Cumberland, the Kentucky, and the Big Sandy worked under the U.M.W. contract, except those in the peripheral counties of Clay and Leslie. If coal had a king in those years, he was not a mogul with diamond rings, lordly mansions, and gleaming trains; he was John Llewellyn Lewis, who commanded a mighty host of disciplined and faithful miners. He loved nothing more than to castigate coal operators for what he perceived as their varied and serious shortcomings. Under "John L." the organization gained the nation's highest wage scale and the first industry-financed health and welfare program. Lewis was dubbed a "labor statesman" by much of the press, and his followers were called the "royalty of American labor." But then the old cycle repeated itself. When World War II was over, the new managers took earnings that the moguls would have distributed as dividends and plowed them into many trainloads of labor-saving machines. As new technology swept into the mines, enormous ships from the Middle East began lining up to disgorge their cheap oil at American docks, most miners lost their jobs, and scores of companies disappeared. The U.M.W. declined and eventually cracked up in corruption, disgrace, dissension, and the horrible murders of the Yablonski family. Since 1959 the eastern Kentucky field has been largely non-union, and members of the U.M.W. now dig less than half the nation's total coal output.[17]

In Harlan labor peace was delayed for half a decade after the coming of the New Deal. The county's mines fell victim to a railroad rate 35 cents per ton higher than those prevailing in competing fields. Because of this "tariff differential," the operators believed they could survive only if they paid wages substantially lower than those offered by their competitors, and for years the Harlan County Coal Operators' Association waged a classic, old-style war to keep out the U.M.W. Defeat came late in the 1930's, when the operators yielded to federal lawsuits and indictments.

Legend has it that militant miners won the struggle in a no-holds-barred confrontation, with the ragged workers overcoming and humbling the "rich and mighty capitalists." In his *Hell in Harlan* George Titler, the U.M.W.'s director of organizing activities, places much of the credit elsewhere—in lawsuits brought by the U.S. Department of Justice under the National Labor Relations Act. Not even the Harlan County Coal Operators' Association with all its gunmen could beat Uncle Sam after the constitutionality of the N.L.R.B. had been sustained by the Supreme Court.[18]

Cleon K. Calvert of Pineville, an attorney for the operators' association during that hectic decade, offered still another explanation. In a conversation thirty years ago he told me that Franklin D. Roosevelt crushed the Harlan operators through the Kentenia Corporation. The leases to the operators had expired or were about to do so, and President Roosevelt persuaded his kinsmen and friends in the company to notify its lessee-operators that unless they made peace with their miners there would be no renewals. The operators, facing the loss of their entire investments, capitulated, and the last major non-union redoubt was organized in 1937. Late in 1941 Myron C. Taylor, U.S. Steel's chief executive officer, worked out a deal with FDR and John L. Lewis that imposed a union-shop contract on all of the company's mines.[19]

Mayo's great friend Johnson Newlon Camden, Sr., was old

when his mine blew up at Monogah. Soon after that experience he resigned from the presidency of Northern Coal & Coke, withdrew from active participation in business affairs, and moved to his retirement home on a Florida island. He died in 1908, partly, at least, because of worry about those myriad deaths and the terrible criticism to which he had been subjected because of them.[20] His son moved to Versailles, Kentucky, in 1892 and lived out his days as a country gentleman in the heart of the Bluegrass region. A graduate of Phillips Academy at Andover, Massachusetts, and of the Virginia Military Institute, Johnson Newlon Camden, Jr., lived quietly on a generous flow of corporate dividends from 1902 until his death in 1942. He served as vice-president of Monogah Coal & Coke Company, vice-president of the $50 million Elk Horn Coal Corporation, and president of the 150,000-acre Kentucky River Coal Corporation, a giant whose holdings have since grown to 190,000 acres. He was a director of three banks in Kentucky and West Virginia, and he organized and largely financed the Camden Interstate Railroad. For four years he was a trustee of the University of Kentucky, and when U.S. Senator William O. Bradley died in 1914, Governor James McCreary appointed Camden to finish the term. From 1920 to 1924 he was a Democratic national committeeman. Camden was chairman of the American Turf Association and of its forerunner, the Jockey Club. He was a member of the Pendennis and River Valley Clubs and of the Metropolitan and University Club of Washington, D.C.[21] The library at Morehead State University bears his name—an honor bestowed by a grateful commonwealth in appreciation of his forgotten statesmanship. (Inquiry on the Morehead campus has failed to turn up anyone with knowledge of the man whose name is so boldly imprinted above the library's entrance.) Camden marshaled the forces that crushed Barkley's gubernatorial bid and sent William Fields of Carter County ("Wild Bill from Olive Hill") to that august office. When Barkley referred to "filthy hands" he had Camden's in mind, having been outwitted and thwarted by the crafty tycoon. Camden preserved his fortune through the Depression and died laden with honor and acclaim.

When the coal boom of World War II was history, when strip-

mining and new technologies became dominant in the pits that
continued to operate despite the competition of floods of foreign oil, the shovelers and timber setters vanished from the tunnels. They vanished from the hills, too, as a million people
moved off to the cities. The showplace town of Lynch, the pride
of the industry in the 1920's, became a white elephant in the
1960's.

Paternalism had not worked. Under the new order a few could
produce more than many could have during the Age of the
Moguls. The men who operated the "continuous miners" de-
rided Lynch's memorable "blue ribbon day" in 1923. U.S. Steel
tore down most of the town. The mammoth tipple was stripped
of its machinery and abandoned. The hotel and boardinghouses
were demolished. The power plant gave up the ghost. The doors
of the great store were boarded up. What was left of the place
was "set free" and became a tiny incorporated village whose
chief worry became the financing of schools for the handful of
children who still lived there.

In 1963 *New York Times* reporter Homer Bigart reached
Lynch while crews labored to remove what other crews had
toiled to construct forty-six years earlier. In telling of the demise
of a town, he told also of the demise of the moguls and the
world they had so imperiously built:

> Unemployment remains high because of automation. At Lynch
> in Harlan County one-third of the city is being demolished by
> United States Coal & Coke Company, a subsidiary of the United
> States Steel Corporation.
>
> The company no longer wants most of the population it had in
> 1960. Whole streets have been torn down. All that remains in the
> upper part of the city are forlorn rows of chimneys, standing like
> artifacts from a forgotten culture.
>
> The company had strip-mined the steep slopes of Big Black
> Mountain behind the town. Deprived of the protective cover of
> forest, the mountainside is exposed to erosion. Last March part
> of the town was inundated by mud slides that ruined homes and
> company facilities, and choked Looney Creek.

Bigart also visited Charles E. Hellier's town sixty years after
the masons and carpenters had left it: "Today the valley resem-
bles a string of ghost towns. The Hellier City Hall is aban-

doned; only a few stores remain. Dirty faced children haul water from the creek, which is befouled with garbage and discarded mattresses."[22] Another scribe who visited Hellier a year or two later described it as a place where a man could sit on his front porch and look across the threshold of hell. It was a town of dilapidated company houses, many of which had been wrecked for firewood; loathsome creeks, unwashed children, poverty, powerlessness, apathy, sickness, and trash abounded. For squalor it could hardly have been equaled in North America—a grim monument to the memory of a genteel New England mogul.[23]

In the late 1940's many companies sold their towns house by house to the miners, jettisoning the old paternalism as a matter of corporate policy. Most houses sold for about $1,000; now, more than thirty years later, they reflect the fortunes and aspirations of the people who bought them. Some were abandoned as new owners flocked to the cities. Others lapsed into wreckage because of neglect. Still others have been much improved with paint, concrete block foundations, aluminum siding, and shingles. The towns the moguls built now stand in their carefully spaced rows, waiting, perhaps, for the moguls to return, and for new turns of Fortune's wheel to restore to them purpose, dignity, and prosperity. Strange things happen in the hills: they may not wait in vain. New moguls, richer than those of yore, may yet come to dig the coal from those ancient beds.

The moguls came to grief because they did not gasp that their world was not as solid as LaGrange, Highgate, Hyde Park, and their other great houses. Like our own tottering economic system, their world was built on paper and credit, and it slid out from under them on an October day in 1929 when terrified multitudes rushed to sell the fancy certificates that "prudent men" had told them were "sound investments." The mines had multiplied almost without number, until the market could not absorb all that coal. Then the houses and tipples and mine shafts and stores, and the men and women who called those places home, became derelict and useless for a time.

The moguls were felled by a blind unwillingness to think in terms of social welfare beyond the corporate paternalism of their own towns. That their workmen and their families had souls and aspirations beyond the coal shovel, kitchen stove, and bean kettle surpassed their understanding. Like Andrew Carnegie, they believed that the lower orders of men and women were "weak and dull-witted," quite content to work and sleep and breed while men of money and sophistication shaped world affairs. Social and cultural revolution swamped this unwisdom.

The moguls were doomed because they refused to make peace with the dust-covered men who made their mines productive. All demands for enhanced living standards, for an end to utter political powerlessness, and for freedom, pure and simple, were met with bland evasions or flinty rejections. The minds of the masses were in ferment while their own heads were locked to all but conservative dogma. They were fortunate to escape 1932 with their lives.

The moguls betrayed the region they industrialized because they never thought beyond the balance sheet. They gave no constructive leadership in the government circles they so effectively dominated. From them came no broad regional plans for good schools, public health programs, industrial diversity, libraries, regional universities, and environmental enhancement. When their paternalistic order collapsed, their miners adopted the union as their staff and comforter. Unionism took on the power of a religion with miners for a quarter-century until the union, too, sank under the impact of technologies that replaced men with machines.

Then the people in those once-magic towns turned to embrace welfarism as a way of life. In the towns the moguls built, the welfare offices now support more people than does the coal industry. Government, left to deal with social and economic problems the moguls shunned, today has become so pervasive that it threatens to stifle the capitalism the moguls loved. By their blindness, greed, and unconcern they set in motion forces that promise to strangle their cherished order of money, privilege, and power.

It is ironic, and perhaps just, that today in the land the moguls invaded and transformed only a few people remember or know about the men who left their names on the map in those strange, stark, frozen towns. The stories behind such places are slipping away unrecorded. Not even the postmasters have heard of the men for whom their locations were named. As if written on the wind, the story of the moguls dies with scarcely a trace.

Perhaps one reason for their unlamented passing was that they were so niggardly toward the region where they had invested so heavily and profited so much. They loved to call themselves philanthropists, and their formal biographical sketches nearly always list the noble endeavors on which they bestowed funds. For example, George Pepper, who owned about 20,000 acres in Letcher County when he died in 1890, used two typewritten pages in his will to enumerate the hospitals, libraries, and other benevolent institutions to which he left substantial bequests—all of them in his home city of Philadelphia. In the hills there are no libraries, parks, hospitals, schools, or scholarships that bear the names of Pepper, Watson, Haymond, Morgan, Fleming, Rockefeller, Eavenson, Westervelt, Whitfield, Payne, Delano, Forbes, Roosevelt, Black, Camden, Mayo, or anyone else of their generations. Their successors have been equally stingy. The whole land therefore lies barren of the cultural facilities without which life must remain relatively sterile and true education impossible.

Their cupidity made the moguls eminently forgettable.

Hellier, Pike County, as it appeared ca. 1970. (Courtesy of Milton Rogovin, Buffalo, N.Y.)

Company store and office building in Stearns, ca. 1980. (Anne F. Caudill.)

Highgate, Fairmont, W. Va., home of James Otis Watson in former days. (Anne F. Caudill.)

Bert Combs. (Courtesy of Louisville *Courier-Journal.*)

William Sturgill. (Courtesy of Louisville *Courier-Journal.*)

Strip-mined land in Knott County, ca. 1970. (Courtesy of Jean Martin, Freeville, N.Y.)

TEN

The Modern Moguls

The masters of the government of the United States are the combined capitalists and manufacturers of the United States. It is
written over every intimate page of the record of Congress, it is
written all through the history of conferences at the White
House, that the suggestions of economic policy in this country
have come from one source, not from many sources. The benevolent guardians, the kind-hearted trustees who have taken the
troubles of government off our hands have become so conspic-
uous that almost anybody can write out a list of them.

Suppose you go to Washington and try to get at your government. You will always find that while you are politely listened
to, the men who are really consulted are the men who have the
biggest stake—the big bankers, the big manufacturers, the big
masters of commerce, the heads of railroad corporations. . . .
The government of the United States at present is a foster child
of the special interests.

—Woodrow Wilson, *The New Freedom* (1913)

IF THE FLAMBOYANT Age of the Moguls died with
Black Friday and the New Deal, what became of the great con-
centrations of power they worked so hard to assemble? Numerous economists, social scientists, and historians from Ferdinand
Lundberg to John Kenneth Galbraith have ridiculed the notion
that a reign of egalitarianism and democracy subsequently descended upon American society. We are, they argue, still a plu-
tocracy. Some say we have the "best Congress money can buy";
the same is true of state legislatures, where eager palms grasp
"campaign contributions." "Big energy"—the conglomerates of
oil, coal, gas, uranium, and chemicals—rule the American roost
as surely as Blackbeard and Captain Kidd once ruled their quar-
terdecks. In Kentucky, Alben Barkley's "coal combine" has be-

come a smooth, solidly entrenched energy combine that operates quietly, cleverly, and almost without challenge. Its power
reaches everywhere. The state exists to serve the purposes of the
new, modern moguls.

I do not contend that the energy concerns in Kentucky and
across the nation operate as tightly controlled, formally structured organizations like John D. Rockefeller's old Standard Oil
trust or the South Improvement Company that preceded it.
Such illegal arrangements have long been outmoded, and in this
sense a Kentucky coal combine probably never existed. However, the same ends can be achieved through more subtle
devices—ends that include acquiring subsidies for beneficial research, for pipelines and refineries, for liquefaction and gasification plants, generous tax laws, and "reasonable" enforcement
of restrictive legislation. The modern energy alliance, tacit
rather than overt, operates through a grand "community of interests." In his *House of Morgan* Lewis Corey attributes to
J. P. Morgan the philosophy of all such combines: "Men own-
ing property should do what they like with it and act toward
mutual harmony."[1]

Kentucky has become the world's fourth- or fifth-largest coal-
producing jurisdiction, depending on whether the discontented
miners of Poland are working or striking. The state's 1981 output of about 155 million tons would suffice to fill a train extending three times from New York to San Francisco. Only the naive
may suppose that the industrial sophisticates who own and
operate Kentucky's energy colossus have failed to generate an
effective community of interests for the imposition of their collective will on the government and people of the weak, archai-
cally structured commonwealth. This chapter will examine Kentucky's immense coal combine or "community of interests" as it
flourishes today.

In the 1980 session of the Kentucky legislature, an educational television station provided Kentuckians with a rare opportunity to observe the men and women who legislate "for the
people." Night after night the camera showed the lawmakers in
action on the floor of the marble-columned chamber. Boredom
was the most common reaction to the sessions, and most view-
ers soon turned to other stations. However, the camera was in-

structive for all who could endure the verbosity and tedium. The poor grammar and atrocious syntax testified to the low quality of the state's educational system, and the persistent public abasement of the lawmakers before the coal industry clearly revealed the locus of real power.

Kentucky has a wretched record in the field of environmental law. It has long been a dumping ground for toxic chemicals; trucks sometimes brazenly pour deadly wastes into city sewers. The Ohio River is a vast ribbon of pollution. In the eastern coal fields the streams reek of every imaginable contaminant, and roadside dumps abound. Such efforts as have been made to clean up the waterways and the atmosphere have come only in response to federal prodding. Six successive governors did little to protect the hills, while strip miners destroyed more than 300,000 acres of needed timberland and permanently (and perhaps ruinously) degraded the water supply of Lexington, the state's fastest-growing and most promising city. Groups of agitated citizens lobbied for strict reclamation laws and stern enforcement, and a few legislators worked hard to help them. But the governors and most lawmakers skillfully ducked the issues.

In 1977 President Jimmy Carter signed a federal mine reclamation law that Gerald Ford had vetoed. It mandated long-needed procedures to assure some future utility for the lands devastated by coal mining and other forms of stripping. Congress authorized the states to adopt laws and regulations conforming with the federal requirements and thereupon to assume primary responsibility for their enforcement. If a reasonable and necessary statute ever found favor in Congress it was that one, as fifteen years of hearings and field trips had made abundantly clear.

In 1980 the Kentucky solons debated a reclamation act—or, more accurately, they postured and ranted in what was supposed to be a debate. (They passed the legislation, of course, because otherwise the hated "feds" would have patrolled the hilltops to see what was being accomplished.) But first the legislators found it necessary to declaim. The voices that might have spoken for the future—for posterity—were still. Advocates of the coming generations who must drink Kentucky water and live by crops and timber drawn from Kentucky soil were mute.

No one protested the ugly scars left on hillsides by contour stripping, or the ghastly stumps that remain in the wake of "mountaintop removal." The land and the future had few supporters in those hallowed halls.

Instead, man after man came to the microphone to lambast those iniquitous feds. The officers were strangling the industry with regulations. Reclamation was not necessary—or not much of it was, anyway. The operators were doing their best and were being very cooperative in "finding solutions." What we need to do, the legislators stressed, is leave them alone and let them mine coal! The operators will free us from bondage to the greedy Arab and Iranian oil potentates!

Jowls quivered as plump young men strove to catch the eyes and gain the favors of the state's coal bosses. None mentioned that, within fifteen months in the 1973–74 spot market, coal producers raised their prices from $8.50 to as much as $80.00 per ton, creating scores of new millionaires in the hills and beginning the impoverishment of millions of electricity consumers. While the "A-rabs" were doubling the price of their crude oil, those American spot marketeers were redoubling the price of their own fuel many times over. Nor did anyone mention that in the same interval the royalties required in new coal leases went up as much as tenfold, to the great benefit of the owners of those old broad-form deeds. While the "energy crisis" induced by the oil embargo gripped the land, coal operators were working around the clock in the best tradition of the old-time moguls to expand their production capacity. By 1978 there was a coal glut. Consumers were buying coal from more dependable suppliers, and a move was underway to gut reclamation laws, loosen air pollution controls, and use federal power to compel electric utility companies to burn coal instead of oil and gas. Most legislators recognized the need for all these steps and told the whole state just how they felt.

A few months later a congressional candidate in eastern Kentucky made the ultimate genuflection before the throne of coal. When a listener asked him what he thought about the problems facing tobacco growers, quick as a wink he retorted: "I am not interested in tobacco farmers. The only people I am interested in is the coal industry!"[2]

These politicians were responding to the power of the combine, that same combine whose "filthy hands" were at Kentucky's throat in 1923. The faces have changed, as have the names of some of the companies. Deaths, inheritances, sales, mergers, and corporate restructurings have reshaped the combine, but its power survives. Now, as then, politicians of both parties seek the favor of coal and its allies and retainers.

Coal's dominance does not lie in the operating companies, even though they have immense influence and no prudent politician will knowingly offend them. Rather, the policymaking power lies in the companies that hold title to eastern Kentucky's veins of coal, its ledges of limestone, its deposits of oil and gas, its subterranean reservoirs of brine, its ores and other minerals. Controlling those, the land companies can specify the terms on which their holdings may be licensed or leased for exploitation. A license is terminable at the will of the land company, and a lease is effective for a specified term. If Cleon Calvert's reminiscence is to be believed, the expiration during the 1930's of leases made in the flush of the town-building era gave Kentenia the power to impose a labor contract on many of Harlan County's tough and bitterly anti-union coal operators. An eastern Kentucky mine owner is doomed if he incurs the wrath of his mineral landlord; he may receive a brief note saying that a change in company policy necessitates cancellation of the license (for which sincere regrets are expressed), or that circumstances beyond its control make the company unable to renew the lease. In the case of small and medium-size mining companies, the landlords like to keep their mining tenants on a "short leash." Hence the letting of relatively small tracts for short terms.

Herein derives the suggestive political power of "the company." A telephone call from a major land company saying that Mr. H. Joseph Blow is a friend of coal and would make a fine legislator carries great weight. "The company says" or "the company wants" are enormously influential utterances. The mine operator will henceforth contribute to Mr. Blow's campaign, urge his employees to vote for him, and attach the candidate's bumper stickers to his cars and trucks. Thus a political nonentity can be converted into the Man of the Hour. When the mining company owns the land it mines, its influence is further magnified because it can participate directly in the anointing of such candidates as Mr. Blow.

The combine is multi-faceted. Its annual coal production has a market value of $5−6 billion and is growing. It extracts approximately 72 billion cubic feet of gas and at least 7 million barrels of high-quality oil, plus a few million tons of sand and crushed limestone. The combine or community of interests consists, first of all, of the land companies which own, in the aggregate, about 1.3 million acres in the Kentucky hills and mountains. These share a common interest with the operating companies whose "royalties" support them. Then come the railroads that haul the coal to market, the chemists whose laboratories analyze it, the brokerage companies that market it, the barge companies that transport it, the electric utilities, the electric cooperatives, and the steel companies that burn it. This vast economic and political muscle is enormously augmented by the supportive oil and gas companies which sink wells into those same lands (and pay royalties for the privilege), the pipeline companies that carry their products to market, and the giant aggregate producers that quarry limestone for roadbuilders and cementmakers. The combine includes the large banks and insurance companies that lend money to the operators, and the small county-seat banks on whose boards the operators serve in goodly numbers.

In Kentucky you see the combine if you want to get any of that political mother's milk of which Jesse Unruh and Lyndon Johnson spoke. When a collector with sound credentials sets out from Ashland, London, Pikeville, or Hazard to call on the friends of coal, he will return with a heavy briefcase. Thereafter favored candidates will suffer from no dearth of television ads and political endorsements, and on election day he will enjoy abundant funding for the numerous "floaters" whose purchased votes can spell victory. Nor is the power of the combine rooted in Appalachia only. The mineral field of western Kentucky is nearly as large and marshals the might of such industrial titans as Texas Gas Transmission Corporation, Peabody Coal, Western Kentucky Coal, Pittsburg & Midway Coal, and the gigantic federally owned electric company called the Tennessee Valley Authority.

The combine was able to defeat Barkley in the 1920's because its money reached into every precinct with payoffs, persuasion, and promises. It still does so today. Consequently a mini-politician from (let us say) Bed Bug Springs, where the major product is broom sedge, may experience the blessings of ample financing if he has proved himself a faithful friend of coal. If he has demonstrated unfriendliness, on the other hand, he is likely to face a well-heeled opponent.

The energy industries' community of interest seeks "friends" who support candidates and policies they deem beneficial: low taxes and as few safety and environmental regulations as possible. If "undue" regulations are nonetheless enacted, the industry favors friendly governors who will enforce them occasionally or not at all. And when mine explosions and other catastrophes occur, they want politicians who will speak up in the industry's defense, assuring the stricken communities that such things are inevitable and represent nothing less than the will of the Almighty. In working for these things by every means at their disposal, today's energy moguls are acting to preserve and enhance profits—a practice as American as apple pie.

The people who hold major stakes in the natural resources of Appalachian Kentucky are numerous, and many of them are obscure. It can be in a wealthy and respected person's best interests to hide his activities behind a bland corporate shield, so that when calamities come the slings and arrows of outrageous fortune will fall upon his tongue-tied professional managers. This was demonstrated in 1972, when a poorly built West Virginia dam collapsed, killing 125 people. Indignation was directed at the president, Nicholas T. Camicia (who began his career as a coal miner), while no one uttered a harsh word about former U. S. Senator Thruston B. Morton, a long-time director and major share owner of Pittston Energy Corporation, the company that created the peril.[3] Likewise, when a mine owned by the Finley brothers blew up on Hurricane Creek in Leslie County in December, 1970, the press pounded the inconsequential Finleys while Henry Ford II, whose Ford Motor Company owned the land, escaped all obloquy.[4] However, enough is known about those who own the region for important insights to emerge. We can identify many people whose decisions largely determine

what the tax levels will be, where roads will be built, which state
reclamation and mine safety laws will be enacted, how they will
be enforced, and in most elections, who will be chosen governor, senator, county judges, and property evaluation admin-
istrators. It is virtually unheard of for a lawyer to reach the federal bench without their quiet approval; if he is to receive the
sanction of governors, senators, and congressmen, he must first
be blessed by the foremost spokemen of coal. Care is taken at all
levels to make sure that only "reasonable" and "safe" men acquire judicial power.

Now let us consider the composition of the combine in the
1980's. Who are the people and the corporations who run Kentucky today, and perhaps for many years to come? Whose political and economic interests interlock to form a "community"?
Who are the moguls now, and who are the brokers and agents
of their power?

In 1956 the Consolidation Coal Company sold most of its
huge holdings in the Elk Horn field to Beth–Elk Horn Corporation, a subsidiary of Bethlehem Steel. By that transaction Bethlehem (company insiders prefer a pronunciation that comes out
"Bethlum") acquired about 104,000 acres. According to Ferdinand Lundberg[5] the purchaser was then dominated to a considerable extent by the descendants of John Davison Rockefeller,
Sr., and his brother William and their banks, foundations, and
trusts. However, by 1980 J. P. Morgan & Company was the
largest shareholder, with 4.73 percent of the stock.[6]

Consolidation Coal retains 28,896 acres of the once vast ter-
ritories it acquired early in the century and it operates a major
mine in Bell County. However, its principal operations are now
in Pennsylvania, West Virginia, Ohio, and the immense new
western fields. World War II made it boom again so that for
a time it owned a controlling interest in the then-prosperous
Chrysler Corporation. It vies with Peabody Coal for the distinc-
tion of being the nation's largest producer. For $670 million it
became a wholly owned subsidiary of Continental Oil (Conoco). In 1981 Conoco and Consol were acquired by E. I. du Pont
de Nemours, the gunpowder and chemical giant. Consol is the
biggest coal producer in West Virginia, where Pendragon's great-

grandson is governor and oversees the destiny of moguls and miners alike.

The Elk Horn Coal Corporation has had an interesting history since its founders passed from the scene. In 1962 it was sold to Ethyl Corporation, a chemical firm that was then owned in equal shares by General Motors and Standard Oil of New Jersey. When GM and Esso ran afoul of the anti-trust laws and were compelled to divest themselves of Ethyl, it was bought by the Albemarle Paper Company of Richmond, Virginia, which was largely the property of a local family named Gottwald. Ethyl's selling price was $238 million, and today Elk Horn is an important part of this huge and growing chemical company. Ethyl stock sells on the New York Stock Exchange, but control and management is securely within the grasp of the Gottwalds. Floyd Gottwald, Jr., a courteous and pragmatic Virginian, has succeeded to the Big Sandy throne once occupied by John Mayo and Clarence Watson. Elk Horn's remaining 134,000 acres lie in four counties and are mined by several major coal firms. "Just a word from Elk Horn" carries immense weight; the discreet and undramatic Gottwald can exert more real power in the Big Sandy than any of the valley's politicians would dare to claim.[7]

The Kentucky River Coal Corporation was being assembled when illness struck Mayo in 1914. After Mayo's death John Buckingham and C. Bascom Slemp, co-executors of his will, completed the formation of that little-known but exceedingly powerful company. Today its 190,000 acres lie in Harlan, Letcher, Perry, Knott, Leslie, and Breathitt Counties, in themselves equaling the territory of a small county. Eighty thousand of those acres are held in fee simple and in the other 110,000 mineral rights are owned as defined and conveyed by Mayo's broadform deed. A post office in Perry County is named for Slemp, who contributed 90,000 acres to the corporation.

The Fairmont entrepreneurs acquired about 16 percent of the stock in Kentucky River Coal for their Elk Horn Coal Corporation. Johnson Newlon Camden, Jr., also invested heavily.[8] Over the years numerous other people acquired small holdings in Kentucky River Coal, but today it remains securely in the hands of heirs—people who inherited broad expanses of land, huge flows of mineral royalties, and a decisive role in regional and state politics. This closely held corporation divulges little information, though available evidence indicates the general outlines of its ownership and profitability.

The Gottwalds managed their 16 percent through Elkhorn Coal until a few years ago, when they sold back their shares to Kentucky River, which acquired them as treasury stock. Their selling price was reportedly higher than had been paid by Ethyl for all of Elk Horn's stock before the Arab oil embargo of 1973. This purchase left the heirs and descendants of John C. C. Mayo, John and Daniel Langhorne (whose Tennis Coal Company was merged into Kentucky River), C. Bascom Slemp, and Johnson N. Camden, Jr., in unassailable dominance, apparently holding some 58,000 of the approximately 83,000 shares now outstanding. The largest aggregations are held by the Langhorne-Bond-Westervelt and Camden-Stoll-Clay family groups. Camden left his huge estate in equal parts to his children and his wife, Agnes. Upon her death her portion of the stock descended to Camden's stepchildren, and one of them, Catesby Woodford Clay of Runnymede Farm in Bourbon County, is now president of the giant.[9] Catesby Clay's standing in the combine is indicated by his board memberships. In addition to Kentucky River Coal, he is a director of Churchill Downs, Grant Coal Company, Abijah Coal Company, P. J. McEvoy, Inc., the Kentucky Coal Association, and the National Council of Coal Lessors. He is president of Grant Coal, Abijah Coal, and Runnymede Farm. He serves as trustee of the Lexington School and of Thomas More College.[10]

As time passes, the owners multiply and the interests of each decline. Still, in an energy-short world the heirs of these fortunate families can look forward to long years of economic security and social respectability. The company made more money in a half-dozen years after 1973 than during its entire previous history, and its prospects are bright. The successive presidents of Kentucky River Coal will be consulted for many decades to come on matters of taxation, gubernatorial and congressional candidates, appointments to the bench and to regulatory boards, selection of university trustees, and the desirability of pending legislation. They could not escape this influence even if they wanted to, for the power that flows from the ownership of such rich and extensive holdings is unavoidably theirs. Only the president of Kentucky's super corporation, Ashland Oil, is likely to be heard with greater respect.

Kentucky River Coal was one of the two companies Thomas Murray described as money wells in a 1965 *Dun's Review* article. The other such firm was Virginia Coal & Iron, since then renamed the Penn Virginia Corporation. Its Kentucky holdings are relatively small (fewer than 5,000 acres) but its influence is immense.[11] It owns more than 150,000 acres in Virginia and West Virginia and is closely tied to rail and utility companies. It is the parent of the huge Westmoreland Coal and Westmoreland Resources. The president of Penn Virginia, Edward Leisenring, is typical of the intelligent, well-educated, immensely powerful and deliberately obscure men who rule modern Appalachia. He does not answer troublesome telephone calls or respond to letters of inquiry, and the *Standard & Poor's Register of Corporations* (1980) gives only the scantiest information about him.[12]

Edward B. Leisenring, Jr., was born in Bryn Mawr, Pennsylvania, in 1926, a scion of coal giants. His ancestors include a founder of Berwind Coal Company; the coal and banking tycoon Israel Platt Pardee, for whom Pardee, Virginia, was named; and Daniel Wentz, whose Wentz Corporation sold to U.S. Steel the land on which Lynch was built. Leisenring's company headquarters are in a modest suite at 123 Broad Street in Philadelphia. His proudest boast is that Penn Virginia has arranged its affairs so ingeniously that almost its entire income is "carried down to net"—that is, tax free for the benefit of Penn Virginia's stockholders. His list of corporate offices reflects the power sources of Appalachia and the manner in which they interlock to form the combine. He is chairman of the board and chief executive officer of Penn Virginia and Westmoreland Coal. He is a member of the executive committee of the Bituminous Coal Operators Association, and he sits on the boards of Whitehall Cement Manufacturing, Norfolk-Southern Railway, General Coal Company, SKF Industries, Fidelity Bank, I U International Corporation, Fidelcor, and Quaker City Insurance Company. He serves as vice-chairman and trustee of Lankenau Hospital, in Pennsylvania.

Though Leisenring stays in the background, his influence should not be underestimated. For example, the Southern Railway provides Kentucky with its most reliable rail service, and Edward Breathitt is a Southern vice-president. A call from Leisenring can send that former Kentucky governor up to Frankfort to "take care" of any "misunderstanding" and prevent any injustice the state might be about to perpetrate. As a lobbyist Breathitt is as smooth as silk; he is also knowledgeable, and knowledge and smooth persuasiveness are a winning combination.

In the 1880's a wealthy New Yorker, Douglas Robinson, employed a lawyer named T. P. Trigg to cross the ridges from his home in the lovely town of Abingdon, Virginia, and buy timber and coal lands. Trigg and his friend W. J. Horsley were men of patience and finesse who acquired about 81,000 acres of mineral rights plus 19,000 acres in fee simple. They operated so adroitly that the sellers never suspected the true identity of the ultimate buyer; instead, they believed they were selling to "gentlemen in Virginia and Tennessee."[13]

Robinson was married to Theodore Roosevelt's sister Corinne. In the early 1890's he sent Teddy's brother, Elliott, down to Abingdon to look after the properties and to speed up the purchases. Elliott was the father of Eleanor, who married her distant cousin Franklin and was America's first lady for twelve years.[14] The Robinson-Roosevelt-Delano syndicate included a number of Virginians. The creation wrought by their labors was given the resounding name of the Virginia Iron, Coal & Coke Company, and the town that grew up in the midst of their mining operations was called Vicco, an acronym. The company is generally known simply as VIC.

VIC's properties in the Kentucky and Big Sandy Valleys rival the vast spreads of Elk Horn Coal and Kentucky River Coal; in addition, there are 87,503 acres in Virginia, 60,517 in Tennessee, 2,501 in Georgia, and 500 in Ashe County, North Carolina. Its total domain in the Appalachians is at least 253,000 acres. In Kentucky a dozen major companies mine its coal.[15] But VIC does not stand alone. It is now one of many energy companies owned by a conglomerate called American Natural Resources Company. To put VIC in perspective, consider some of the others: Michigan Wisconsin Pipe Line Company, ANG Coal Gasification Company, ANR Coal Company, ANR Western Coal Development Company, and American Natural Offshore Company.

The president of American Natural Resources is Arthur R. Seder, Jr., a genial Michigander. His board is composed of Canadians and Midwesterners who are directors of a broad range of other U.S. firms, including Jeep Corporation, American Motors General Corporation, United States Trust Company, Chrysler Corporation, National Bank of Detroit, Grand Trunk Western Railroad, and Atlantic Mutual Insurance Company. These directors are graduates of Yale, Stanford, the University of Alberta, Massachusetts Institute of Technology, the University of Connecticut, the University of Detroit, and the University of Michigan. Their memberships include the Council on Foreign Relations, Association of Reserve City Bankers, American Society for International Law, and the Atlantic Council of the United States.

The political and economic influence of this energy giant is almost beyond measure. It extends into many states and the District of Columbia and has its retainers and allies in each of them. In Kentucky its capacity to get things done is incalculable.[16]

Armand Hammer, chairman of Occidental Petroleum, is an old-style super-mogul. His oil giant owns Hooker Chemical, which won worldwide recognition for burying vast quantities of deadly chemical wastes at Love Canal near Niagara Falls, New York. His gigantic Island Creek Coal Company is wholly owned by Occidental and is Kentucky's second-largest producer; its holdings there cover 112,108 acres.[17] Hammer's Kentucky surrogate is Albert Gore, board chairman of Island Creek Coal, who in the 1960's was a vocal liberal senator from Tennessee. His son is a congressman. The ex-senator strives to see that Kentucky and federal officials lay no undue burdens on the company.

In March, 1980, Royal Dutch Shell invested $680 million in coal lands and mining facilities in Tennessee, West Virginia, Kentucky, and Colorado. Royal Dutch is the world's second-largest oil company and employs a thousand miners in Martin and Pike Counties.[18]

The railroads, too, are mineral landlords on a mammoth scale. In 1980 Norfolk & Western (now Norfolk-Southern Corporation) bought Kentenia, the Harlan giant, in an acquisition that brought its holdings in Kentucky to at least 130,000 acres, including half of Martin County. Chessie Systems (formerly the Chesapeake & Ohio) owns another 59,000 acres.

When Ferdinand Lundberg described America's wealthiest families,[19] he listed three Berwinds among the country's top money elite. Their giant fortune was made in the Berwind-White Coal Company in Pennsylvania. The Berwind Corporation owns 80,000 acres which were purchased by John C. C. Mayo, and the company has funneled royalties and dividends to the hereditary owners in Philadelphia for nearly seventy years.

The Pittston Company owns Kentland–Elk Horn Coal Corporation and Eastern Coal Corporation and their mines and tipples. These subsidiaries operate on thousands of acres of prime coal, oil, and gas land owned by Berwind-White. Pittston owns in fee simple 275,163 additional acres in Virginia and West Virginia, and its board often displays the names of Mortons. Thruston B. Morton, the former senator from Kentucky, and Rogers C. B. Morton, his brother and cabinet member under Richard Nixon, were long prominent in its affairs. Pittston operates forty-three mines with a combined capacity of about 16 million tons annually. Its subsidiaries include Brink's, the armored truck company. In 1971 Joseph Routh, then chairman of Pittston's board of directors, gave Cornell University $350,000 to buy artificial turf for its football field. In contrast, gifts by Pittston and its officers to Kentucky schools have been scanty and few.[20]

The hereditary nature of coal's power and money is illustrated by the Calvin Corporation. Its headquarters are in Philadelphia and it owns 6,037 acres of Kentucky's finest Elk Horn coal. This relatively small leasing corporation was named for its founder, Calvin Nathaniel Payne, a hard-bitten Standard Oil pirate who was a brilliant petroleum engineer during the industry's infancy and upon whom Pendragon relied in both technical and managerial matters.[21] His descendants draw what Kyle Vance described as a "river of profit" from this corporation and from the Big Sandy Company. The chairman of the latter is an imperious Boston tycoon named Nelson Darling.

A trust fund managed by Commerce Union Bank of Nashville, Tennessee, for the heirs of Justin Potter controls 75,309 acres of eastern Kentucky land. The Tennessee Valley Authority owns 71,601 acres. A corporate syndicate composed of Williams Energy, Newmont Mining, Equitable Life & Casualty Insurance, Bechtel International Corporation, Fluor Corporation, and Boeing owns Peabody Coal, which, in turn, owns 20,008 acres.[22]

Blue Diamond Coal Company owns 34,118 acres and in a single year (fiscal 1975) increased its cash and marketable securities by $55.6 million, leading it to be described by *Forbes* as "swimming in prosperity."[23] Gordon Bonnyman, the modest Princetonian who runs Blue Diamond, is a mogul in every sense of the word but is almost invisible. In addition to its other assets, Blue Diamond owns at least 5.4 million shares of McLouth Steel Corporation.

Stearns Coal & Timber has kept its title to approximately 100,000 acres of mineral rights. In the 1930's the company sold most of the surface to the federal government, and it now lies within the Daniel Boone National Forest. Stearns has brought a suit in federal court at Lexington seeking authority to strip mine the land. If the company wins, one of the loveliest and most productive of the nation's publicly owned woodlands will be devastated by a mining procedure called "mountaintop removal and hollow fill."

Perhaps two of the owners of eastern Kentucky should be called "academic moguls": the holdings of Harvard and Princeton universities total 9,862 acres.[24]

National Steel holds 21,000 acres and has a large, modern mine in Knott County. By inheritance from M. A. Hanna and his brother, Howard, Kate Ireland is a major stockholder of this important steel producer. Miss Ireland has spent her life as a Frontier Nursing Service administrator in the Leslie County backwoods. Though few of her neighbors have an inkling of it, she is a woman of great influence; she is a partner in the prestigious Wall Street firm of Brown Brothers, Harriman & Company and her listed business address is 1010 Hanna Building, Cleveland. She is a generous donor to conservative Republican politicians and has much influence in the Kentucky GOP. Knowledgeable politicos have credited her with quietly engineering the event that brought Richard Nixon from California to speak at the county-seat town of Hyden in 1978, in his first significant public appearance after his resignation from the presidency. Her political contributions in 1979–80 totaled $16,000.[25]

Other major owners of the eastern Kentucky mineral fields and their respective acreages include: Warfork Land Company, 25,584; Kycoga Corporation, 40,000; United States Steel, 41,000; International Harvester, 6,800; Ford Motor Company, 13,800; U.S. Plywood-Champion Papers, 24,000; Duke Power, 13,300; Georgia Pacific, 11,000; Alcoa, 10,700; and Republic Steel, 5,134.[26]

The economic fulcrum that controls and directs coal appears to be slowly shifting from Boston, Philadelphia, and New York to a new center in Houston. Coal is being absorbed by oil as the petroleum companies become energy conglomerates producing a varied mix of fuels. In 1978 J. M. Huber Corporation bought the 80,000 acres left to the American Association after the long-ago Middlesboro debacle. Kaneb Services, Diamond Shamrock, Mapco, and Ashland Oil exemplify companies which have used their "energy crisis" profits to develop coal mines and gas wells.[27]

Big oil looms ever larger and more compelling in the councils of the combine. Money flowing up from Houston now blesses many candidates for public office, as was illustrated in the 1978 election of Congressman Larry Hopkins in a Kentucky district utterly without coal mines or oil wells. The political action committees of oil, coal, and steel corporations sent him gifts totaling at least $14,000.[28]

Some of the oil moguls who benefit from Kentucky's mineral deposits are breathtakingly rich. Pittsburg Midway Coal, an immense stripper, is a Gulf Oil subsidiary. Gulf is one of the "seven sisters" that dominate the international oil trade, and 20 percent of its stock (39 million shares) is owned by the Mellon family, their foundations and trusts, and Mellon National Corporation.[29]

Big gas, too, is a huge participant in the combine, drawing its product silently out of the same acres that those luckless mountaineers sold to John C. C. Mayo and other "developers." The phony gas crisis of the early 1970's produced partial deregulation followed by immense price increases at the wellhead; this resulted in new drilling and the reactivation of many capped and previously unproductive wells. There are now more than 4,500 wells in the hills, most of them on land owned by or leased to three major companies. Equitable Gas Company is the largest, with 975,000 acres under lease. Ashland Oil (high on the list of *Fortune*'s 500 largest corporations) has 320,000 acres, and Columbia Gas Company another 281,000. Edward Wilson, who from 1965 to 1976 directed the Oil and Gas Division of the Kentucky Geological Survey, has estimated that Kentucky's proven reserves contain about 500 billion cubic feet of the fuel.[30]

In social and economic terms there are two Appalachias. One is made up of the people who live there, a few of whom are wealthy and the rest poor by national standards. The other, the corporate Appalachia of the combine, is very, very rich. Some of the inhabitants are united by economic ties to the corporate Appalachia; they lease coal from the land companies, work in the mines, service its oil and gas wells, keep records for the companies, and provide legal counsel. But they are few in overall terms. The others are pupils and schoolteachers, state and federal workers, the unemployed, and public assistance recipients.

Eastern Kentucky is a colony owned and managed by absentee landlords. When the mineral deeds were signed, sovereignty passed to a class of wealthy, distant, and aloof people. They have demonstrated a chilling unconcern for the region during the eighty years since a colonial status was imposed on an ignorant and gullible population.[31] Today's mineral landlords, like their predecessors, provide no leadership in solving the state's problems. Instead, they so burden and oppress beautiful, resource-rich Kentucky that it is backward and impoverished: in 1976 its per capita income lagged behind that of Iceland.[32]

Confronted by social and economic lags in Libya or Saudi Arabia, American industrialists pour out technological and scientific marvels to maintain the good will of kings and dictators. In Libya, for example, Occidental Petroleum (parent of Island Creek Coal) found enormous aquifers, enabling thousands of acres of the world's bleakest desert to become fruitful. In Kentucky, meanwhile, the same corporation ignores social and economic problems that have plagued the mountains for generations. The Appalachian mineral fields are the only colonial territory where officials are still routinely elected by the subject population because they have promised to serve the absentee rulers!

The power of the combine in the 1980's is shown by the career of William Sturgill. If anyone in the state deserves to be called "Mr. Coal" it is he, though "Mr. Kentucky" might be more appropriate. Sturgill is almost certainly the most powerful Kentuckian, with influence that reaches into coal, oil, gas, insurance, banking, tobacco, construction, real estate development, fertilizer, higher education, and railroads. He listens to the mineral overlords, and they listen to him. He has been subjected to severe and prolonged criticism in the media and has survived unscathed. His strip mines produced landslides that wrecked houses; an aged woman from Knott County told Governor Edward Breathitt that Sturgill's bulldozers shoved the coffins of her children down a slope, then reburied them under the tumbling spoil. In some parts of the country these acts would have devastated the image of a public figure, but in Kentucky they were shrugged off.

William Sturgill is a mountaineer who moved into the prevailing power structure and captured control of much of it through sheer drive, persistence, and cunning. He grew rich during the coal depression of the 1950's, when scores of his fellow operators were going bankrupt. Today, though relatively few Kentuckians know him, virtually all are affected by his decisions.

He grew up at Prestonsburg, the son of an able Democratic politician. After studying at the University of Kentucky he dropped out of law school and got a job selling explosives for Atlas Powder Company. He then moved to Perry County and became secretary for the Hazard Coal Operators' Association— a position with little pay but much influence. In 1955 he bucked the economic tide and rented an old and dilapidated tipple at Allais, in a dreary Perry County hollow. Two years later his friend Harry LaViers, Jr., president of the South-East Coal Company, loaned him $5,000. A few months later Sturgill was shipping twenty cars of coal daily from two tipples that had been left idle by failed companies.

He bought a home and found a partner, Richard Kelly. Their Knott Coal Company was innovative, relying on augering and contour stripping; its "Kelly Giant" was the largest coal auger in the world at the time, with a seven-foot blade that could penetrate 100 feet into a seam and dig 4,600 tons in ten hours. Although local people protested the noise, the blasting, the landslides, the flooding caused by denuding of the steep slopes, and the ruining of their roads by overloaded coal trucks, their protests were to no avail. The governors heard the complaints but heeded Sturgill, who characterized the critics as "emotional" and the floods as "acts of God."

In 1970 Sturgill and Kelly sold their operation to a Texas oil corporation, Falcon Seabord, for $10.5 million. Sturgill moved to Lexington, where he could operate on a broader scale. He maintained his friendships with the land companies—Elk Horn Coal, Kycoga, Kentucky River, VIC and all the rest—and with the mining companies, meanwhile branching out as opportunity allowed.

In due time he returned to the hills as a strip miner, motivated, no doubt, by a desire to help solve the "energy shortage" and to thwart the Arabs. In 1980 his four tipples in Knott and Letcher Counties shipped trainloads of coal to such customers as American Electric Power and Illinois Power Company. He flew to the hills in his private airplane to check on his wells and mines; the gas from the former went to Columbia Gas, and the oil was bought by Ashland. Then, in December, he sold his Golden Oak Mining Company to a Houston energy firm, Reading and Bates, for $14.3 million.

A few years earlier Sturgill sold the huge Sterling Hardware Company at Hazard, and he no longer owns radio stations WKIC-AM and WSGS-FM, but he still owns five tobacco warehouses, five fertilizer plants, and a county-seat bank in Marion County.

Sturgill is both a generator and a conduit of power. He can initiate or prevent change in many fields, and through him the modern combine transmits its desires to governors, bureaucrats, legislators, and even presidents. In Lexington, "the coal capital of America," he is secretary of the Fayette County Urban Airport Authority. He is a trustee of the Appalachian Regional Hospitals, those same hospitals which once were the proudest achievement of John L. Lewis and the United Mine Workers. He is a director of the First Security National Bank and Trust Company of Lexington, and of Flat Top Insurance Agency of Bluefield, West Virginia. He is chairman of the Kentucky State Racing Commission, president of the Thoroughbred Council of the Boy Scouts of America, and a faithful member of the Lexington Rotary Club. An elder of the Crestwood Christian Church, he is also chairman of its finance committee. He is a member of the Idle Hour Country Club and a director of the Lafayette Club. His income has been estimated at a million dollars annually.[33]

Sturgill is a trustee of Lee's Junior College at Jackson and president of the Hazard Independent College Foundation. As chairman of the Board of Trustees of the University of Kentucky, he writes the agenda for its meetings and keeps a careful eye on its millions of dollars worth of research in medicine, mining, and tobacco. He is also a director of CSX Corporation, the rail titan whose 27,000 miles of track include such subsidiaries as Seaboard Coast Line, the Louisville & Nashville, and the Chessie System. A fellow board member is Floyd Gottwald, Jr., of Ethyl Corporation and Elk Horn Coal.

When a new governor was inaugurated in January, 1980, he appointed a state secretary of energy to protect the people's interests, calling the appointment of William Sturgill the "keystone" of his administration.[34]

Though Sturgill's power and influence are immense, it is doubtful that they much exceed those of his onetime neighbor Bert Combs. This hill-country lawyer turned power broker was born in Clay County, which Rena Gazaway made famous in her classic study of the dependent mountain poor people.[35] Though Combs's mountain drawl and conservative blue shirts and suits disguise him as just a country boy who moved off to Louisville to practice law, he sits near the summit of power as an attorney for the combine.

Combs's boyhood was poor and hard but his subsequent rise was spectacular. Born in 1911, he was an excellent student in Clay County's primitive schools and distinguished himself at the University of Kentucky, graduating from its law school in 1937. He was recruited by Jack Howard of Prestonsburg, the chief counsel for Elk Horn Coal. With Howard's clever support, Combs began a steady climb to money and power.

During World War II another Prestonsburger, A. J. May, was chairman of the House committee on military affairs. When Combs entered the army after Pearl Harbor, May arranged for him to serve on General Douglas MacArthur's legal staff. His duties included gathering evidence against Japanese war criminals; his most prominent victim was Field Marshal Tomoyuki Yamashita, whom a court of victorious American army officers convicted and executed in 1946.

Back in Prestonsburg after the war, Combs was elected commonwealth attorney. When Judge Roy Helm of the Kentucky Court of Appeals died of a heart attack, the adroit Howard induced Governor Lawrence Wetherby to appoint Combs to the vacancy. In 1955 the combine persuaded Wetherby that Combs should be the administration's gubernatorial candidate. His amply financed campaign was thwarted by the redoubtable A. B. "Happy" Chandler, and Combs (whom Happy always referred to as "the little judge") went back to the hills to bide his time. In 1959 Howard convinced the coal interests that Combs deserved support in a second effort, and that time its money and Chandler's unpopularity carried him to victory. Former Senator and Governor Earle Clements wrought a political miracle that put Combs and Wilson Wyatt of Louisville on the same ticket. Wyatt, the candidate for lieutenant governor, owned tens of thousands of acres in Tennessee;[36] he was the darling of such "left-wingers" as Kentucky possessed, meaning that he was only a little to the right of center. Because Wyatt was closely allied to the Bingham family and its influential newspapers and television stations, they sold Combs and Wyatt to the voters as paragons of progressive virtue.

Governor Combs financed a major and badly needed school improvement program with a general retail sales tax, a levy that spared the combine the inconveniences of a severance tax on minerals. The tax exempted all supplies and machines used in mining and drilling, except for those hand tools bought by miners themselves. These latter were duly taxed at 3 percent.

Combs's term ended in 1963, and in 1967 the combine induced President Lyndon B. Johnson to appoint him to the U.S. Court of Appeals in Cincinnati. There, in one of the best deeds of his career, Combs wrote an opinion holding unconstitutional

Kentucky's antiquated criminal syndicalism statute, a law that had long been used to harass and imprison labor organizers and similar "radicals." His judicial opinions were cautious, well-reasoned, and refreshingly progressive.

In 1971 Combs left the bench to run again for governor. He was almost pathetically out of touch with political reality, largely ignoring television and leaving the medium to his younger opponent, Wendell Ford. Furthermore, he openly toyed with the notion of imposing a mineral severance tax—a possibility that was anathema to the energy tycoons.

The disastrous results in the polling booths eventually became Combs's financial blessing. This time he joined a venerable Louisville law firm which was renamed Tarrant, Combs & Bullitt. His faithful friend Jack Howard had died, but all his old contacts with the combine survived. "The judge's" posh office became the unofficial headquarters of a large segment of the combine as Combs and his associates obtained profitable decisions from state regulatory agencies, lobbied the legislators, and finessed the governors. Here arrangements were made for "sensible" appointments to boards and agencies, rising politicians were identified and promoted, and defenses in troublesome lawsuits were devised. In 1980 the Combs firm and that of his old political ally, Wilson Wyatt, were merged into Kentucky's prestigious superfirm. Their clientele is replete with names from the combine: Ashland Oil, Ford Motor Company, South-East Coal, Reynolds Metals, du Pont, Arco, Shell, Southern Railway, Falcon Coal, Blue Diamond Coal, Turner–Elk Horn Mining, Hazard Coal Operators' Association, and a roster of tobacco, distilling, airline, and insurance giants.[37]

Combs has come a long way since his days as a toddler on a Clay County hillside. He is a durable figure who has survived many ups and downs, and his capacity for work is legendary. In Kentucky there is an oft-heard expression: "If Bill can't do it, call Bert." In the field of civil law he can probably deliver more than any other lawyer in the state.

Back in 1967 Combs did a strange thing that must have shocked the combine but for which they generously forgave him. In New York to address a meeting of the Presbyterian Board of National Missions, he spoke with surprising candor and clarity about the social and economic difficulties of the Kentucky hills. Poverty was then in vogue, and Combs expounded on its sources in Appalachia. He described the region as "an underdeveloped area where unemployment and poverty are a way of life. For half a century," he continued, "we have permitted conditions to exist which have created the Appalachian problem. The area has been ruthlessly exploited. The valuable natural resources of the region have been pillaged by those whose only motive was financial profit." The former governor allowed that education was the solution, but first poverty had to be eliminated and the people made healthy. He warmed the hearts of his listeners by saying, "You cannot educate a hungry child, nor a sick child." [38]

Thus in a few sentences Combs described the moguls, their works, and their motives. No other commentator has said it so succinctly. Unfortunately, there is no evidence that he ever returned to the theme of that speech in any subsequent utterance.

(As this is being written, in November 1982, Combs is quite obviously conducting a carefully orchestrated campaign to elect his son-in-law, Bill Weinberg of Hindman, as Kentucky's attorney general, and to promote his friend Harvey Sloane, mayor of Louisville and a millionaire by inheritance, to the governorship. If he succeeds in these efforts, Combs is virtually certain to emerge as the Bluegrass State's dominant power broker, with influence greatly exceeding that of any other individual in the commonwealth.)

A decade later, Howard Fineman of the *Louisville Courier-Journal* interviewed Herbert Lannon, an attorney for the Payne heirs who own a substantial part of eastern Kentucky's mineral wealth. The salaries paid to the state's teachers were next to the lowest in the nation. Eastern Kentucky's roads had been pulverized by coal trucks so that an estimated $2 billion in repairs were needed. Public health was abysmally poor. Lannon ignored all these problems in speaking of the responsibilities and goals of his company: "We're strictly in it for royalties." [39] His statement was chillingly truthful. The moguls of today, steadfastly following the example of their predecessors, bestow few or no benefits on the region. There are no Morton libraries, no American Natural Resources scholarships, no Armand Hammer art museums, no coal-sponsored medical research into the diseases and afflictions of coal miners. With the exceptions of Ashland Oil and Kentucky River Coal, their names never appear as sponsors on Kentucky's educational television network. For years the idea of a museum reflecting the rich cultural heritage of the hill people and the history of the coal industry has been under discussion, but the combine has declined to finance it. As far as the coal fields are concerned, the principle and practice of philanthropy are alien to Kentucky's mineral landlords. Since corporate Appalachia possesses almost all the region's financial resources, there is no hope for such projects without money and leadership from the great corporations.

The power of the combine is best demonstrated in taxes, those troublesome levies that Justice Oliver Wendell Holmes characterized as the price we pay for civilization. In 1972 the huge Ford holdings paid the state and counties an average of 11 cents per acre. Today the state taxes coal *in situ* at the rate of 1/10 cent per $100 of assessed valuation, while other real estate (such as a miner's mortgaged home) may pay 31½ cents.

The combine's respectability is shown by its association with higher education. The mineral overlords love to meet at the burnished tables of the trustees, then adjourn to football and basketball games and the postgame cocktail parties. If a trustee is photographed with a winning team or a heroic coach, the fans in the hinterlands glow with admiration and envy.

Sturgill's accomplishments in higher education have already been noted; brief mention should be made of those of a few of his coal industry compatriots. Since he came from Texas to direct Falcon Coal's Kentucky operations, J. L. Jackson has been wooed and won for the board of Berea College. L. D. Gorman of Hazard, an ultra-conservative coal tycoon with vast acreages in the Hazard field, served a term with Sturgill on the board of trustees of the University of Kentucky. W. T. Young, a distinguished former director of Kaneb Services (the energy giant whose subsidiary, LeeCo, is demolishing many Kentucky hills), was for years a trustee of both the University of Kentucky and prestigious Transylvania College. Cloyd McDowell is a trustee of Morehead State University and president of the Independent Coal Operators' Association. Henry Stratton of Pikeville, a lawyer, banker, and owner by inheritance of extensive mineral lands, long contributed wisdom to the management of Eastern Kentucky University at Richmond. (Stratton once objected to the granting of an honorary degree on the grounds that the proposed recipient was "controversial.")

Although such men make little contribution to any aspect of higher education, they are routinely appointed and reappointed. Why? They are small-town and country figures who are known to be wealthy in their own rights, or to be agents for large and wealthy corporations. Because they share the values of the small-town lawyers who serve as the state's governors, the governor (whoever he is) is comfortable with them. A governor or a university president may even be allowed to participate with the moguls in profitable mineral deals. The name of a prominent educator on a corporate board can bring luster to a firm whose activities are sometimes suspect or even unseemly.

Jesse Stuart is a world-famous Kentucky author who has been the state's poet laureate since 1954, and Wendell Berry is one of the nation's foremost writers about the land and general environmental issues. Each of them is well respected in the nation's literary circles. However, it probably has never occurred to a Kentucky governor to appoint either man to a trusteeship. When this matter was brought up with a battle-wise state senator, he reflected on it for some time before answering. Finally, lighting a fresh cigar, he ventured an opinion: "Well, I guess Berry and Stuart are out because they don't have any coal mines, banks, or supermarket chains. They can't be appointed unless they catch the governor's eye, and they can't catch it if they don't have a lot of money!"

The utter impotence of the general population was demonstrated on July 8, 1980, when Governor John Young Brown, Jr., appointed members of the state's Council on Higher Education. This immensely important agency formulates policy for the state's eight universities and numerous community colleges. After removing the university presidents from the council, Governor Brown reconstituted the membership and charged it with responsibility for reshaping the state's program of higher education during a decade that is expected to see a 20 percent decline in college enrollment. Of his fourteen appointees, seven were lawyers (including Bert Combs), one was the wife of a lawyer, and another was a law student. Four of the appointees were from Louisville, three from Lexington, and three from cities in western Kentucky. The only educator was Carolyn Wosoba, superintendent of schools in a tiny independent district in Jefferson County. All of eastern Kentucky's million residents were represented by Harry LaViers, Jr., president of South-East Coal Company, and Orin Atkins, chairman of the board of Ashland Oil, parent company of the huge coal stripper Addington Brothers Coal Company. (This oil giant is the world's only globe-girdling multi-national hillbilly corporate conglomerate.) No other segment of the population was consulted or even considered. Labor, agriculture, medicine, and primary and secondary education were ignored. Higher education was entrusted to coal and lawyers. The general public was excluded—except, of course, for the duty to pay taxes.[40]

Harry LaViers, Jr., is probably the best-educated and most progressive and humane coal operator in the state. Mine safety is almost a religion with him, and he enjoys good labor relations with his employees. Notwithstanding his relatively liberal record, the most diligent inquiry failed to disclose that either he or Atkins had, up to that time, displayed any concern for education in Kentucky.

However, each has long been a substantial contributor to campaign funds. Atkins has distinguished himself in this respect perhaps more than any other American. On July 9, 1980, the *Wall Street Journal* referred to his triumphs as a political financier. It seems that between 1967 and 1972 he authorized $600,000 in illegal gifts of Ashland's money to politicians. This generosity resulted in federal fines and a suit by indignant stockholders. (Atkins repaid the company $175,000 out of his personal resources and attempted to treat it as a tax-deductible expense; to its credit, the Internal Revenue Service disallowed the deduction.) One can surmise that Ashland's generosity will continue and that, in consequence, Atkins and those who follow him at Ashland's helm will be called upon to contribute counsel to Kentucky's ruling statesmen.

Ashland possesses truly magnificent resources upon which to draw for such purposes. On May 28, 1981, the *Wall Street Jour-*

nal reported that the oil giant's subsidiary, Ashland Coal, had arranged to sell a 25 percent interest in its properties and operations to Saarbergwerke AG for $102.5 million. Saarbergwerke is owned 74 percent by the Federal Republic of Germany and 24 percent by the state of Saarland. A company owned by the Spanish government acquired a 10 percent interest in 1982.

In September, 1980, Ashland Oil did something virtually without precedent among Kentucky's ruling mineral oligarchy. The petroleum behemoth donated $1 million to the University of Kentucky to finance improvement of its College of Business. It also pledged annual gifts of $100,000 to establish visiting professorships in several academic fields, and then William Sturgill gave the university $400,000. A year later, after a series of spectacular and deadly explosions in the state's underground mines, Kentucky River Coal announced a substantial gift to the university's unaccredited School of Mines and Minerals, on condition that other energy companies give comparable sums.

Ashland is not alone in bestowing largesse. On September 29, 1980, when Governor Brown (a fried-chicken tycoon) and his wife were concluding a ten-day European vacation, it happened that Diamond Shamrock had an empty jet ready to leave for the States. The governor and first lady were flown in privacy and comfort, free of charge, to Louisville. Diamond Shamrock owns Falcon Coal, which is strip mining vast districts in eastern Kentucky. State officials regulate Falcon's operations to see that the mined lands are reclaimed. The governor saw no conflict of interest in accepting Diamond Shamrock's trans-Atlantic airlift; rather, he saw his close association with this member of the combine as desirable, affording him flexibility in dealing with the state's business interests. ("A governor has to have flexibility to operate effectively," he explained.[41]) The combine, for its part, would wholeheartedly agree that a flexible governor is highly desirable.

The combine's ingenuity in rewarding its official servitors is boundless. For example, before the 1980 election the Kentucky coal industry staged a $125-per-plate "appreciation dinner" for Senator Wendell Ford. Chairman and co-chairman of the affair were William Sturgill and Bert Combs.[42] A spokesman for the *Kentucky Coal Journal* explained, "The man has done a hell of a lot for the coal industry since he has been in Washington." Ford, a Democrat who was running virtually without Republican opposition, had already received $216,000 for his non-campaign. His heart warmed by the generosity of the moguls, he declared, "I'm going to take it, and I'm glad they're doing it, and I hope we'll have more, because that means I'm doing the right thing."[43] The *Lexington Herald-Leader* referred to Ford as "the Senator from Coal."

On February 1, 1981, Governor Brown spoke at Henderson, Kentucky, in a ceremony dedicating Peabody Coal's grand new office building. The giant mining firm provides 5,500 jobs in Kentucky. According to an Associated Press report in the *Louisville Courier-Journal* the next day, Brown declared, "When Peabody calls, the governor goes." In the fullness of time Kentucky had produced a politician of splendid candor.

The companies that own and pillage eastern Kentucky for financial profit are themselves owned and controlled. A look at some of those "owners of the owners" will illustrate the complexity of the ruling community of interests. Mellon National Corporation owns 314,538 shares of National Steel and 340,511 shares of Diamond Shamrock. It also owns 3,902,127 shares in Gulf Oil (owner of Pittsburg & Midway Coal Company) and 448,106 shares in U.S. Steel, which continues to operate Kentucky's largest deep mine at Lynch. U.S. Steel, in turn, is controlled by the same friendly financial institutions which own its stock as follows: J. P. Morgan & Co., 2,190,000 shares; du Pont family interest, 1,142,668 shares; Manufacturers Hanover Trust, 1,067,680 shares; Lord Abbett & Co., 952,100 shares; and Wells Fargo & Company 266,784 shares. (J. P. Morgan & Co. votes as trustee 11,299,449 additional shares owned by U.S. Steel and Carnegie pension trusts.)

Not to be outdone at the stockholding game, U.S. Steel owns 432,000 shares of Duke Power, 208,302 shares of du Pont, 909,000 shares of Gulf Oil, 41,900 shares of National Steel, and 630,500 shares of Standard Oil Company of Indiana—which is sole owner of Harbert Mining Company, one of eastern Kentucky's largest and most profitable coal strippers.[44]

Binding the energy giants in still closer affinity is the fact that the CSX and the Southern, the railroads that haul the region's

coal to market, are owned largely by the same consortium of
financial institutions. So is American Electric Power Company,
parent of Kentucky Power, the region's largest supplier of electricity. Similarly, the *Wall Street Journal* reported on July 24,
1981, that when du Pont bought Conoco, the same lineup of financial institutions owned both parties to the deal.[45]

If the outlook for the energy tycoons is rosy, the prospects for
eastern Kentucky and the people who live there are chilling. The
fate that awaits them may be one that will eventually befall the
rest of the world, as mankind digs ever more frantically for raw
materials.

From the Big Sandy River westward almost to the Bluegrass
and from the Ohio southward to Virginia and Tennessee, the
Kentucky hills are layered with seams of coal. The power plants
that will burn it by hundreds of tons per minute are already operating or under construction in the Ohio Valley, Europe, and
Japan. Much of the coal in those hard veins will be wrested
from the earth and burned before today's kindergarten pupils
celebrate their fiftieth birthdays. The hilltops will be shaved
away, and the rubble that was once mossy stone and forest floor
will be compacted to fill the hollows. While the resulting mesas
may or may not be "reclaimed" (depending on national whim
or policy), attempts at reclamation are not likely to matter very
much in any event. The bulldozers will return time and again,
and those man-made mesas will be reduced again and again as
lower veins are blasted out and "recovered." When the once-
verdant hills and valleys are jumbled spoil, the rains will carve
new streambeds across the wreckage. The rivers that flow out of
this ruined land will carry colossal cargoes of mud and minerals
to plague the lives and homes of tens of millions of people.

Nor will the assaults end with the leveling of hills and the filling of valleys. Men and long-wall mining machines will continue to burrow until the broken hills crash downward into the
voids. Beset from above and below, the earth will sink into a
desolation that will reduce to relative insignificance the kind of
catastrophe that was inflicted on Flanders during World War I.
This new desert will be dotted with occasional drab towns,
oases for the technicians and workers who will operate the coal
mines, railroads, gas and oil wells, and pipelines. The rest of the

hill people will flee. These descendants of pioneers whose culture still reflects many of the mores and folkways of the frontier will sell their shotguns and hound dogs and slip away to the cities. Some will find work in the robotized factories of the future, while the rest will settle down in deteriorating housing projects to draw welfare checks and collect food stamps, to breed, and to swallow Valium and other "nerve pills."

Lest I be called a prophet of doom and gloom, let me hasten to add that I am not the first to paint this somber picture of the future. The region's doom is virtually sealed: the insatiable global demands for fuel and chemicals have already determined that.

There is a major eastern Kentucky coal operator whose ancestors have lived in the hills for many generations. He is a thoughtful, articulate, and reflective man with an engineering degree from an Ivy League university. Like the men who work in his mines, like those who illuminate their homes with the power from the coal his miners dig, like the directors of Robeco and Chase Manhattan, like all mankind, he is locked into an industrial system he deems unstoppable. "I wish it could be avoided," he said wistfully, "but it cannot. Only God could stop it with a miracle, and I do not believe in miracles."

Notes

Introduction

1. Robert M. Ireland, *Little Kingdoms: The Counties of Kentucky, 1850-1891* (Lexington: University Press of Kentucky, 1977), pp. 60–70.

2. Will Wallace Harney, "A Strange Land and a Peculiar People," *Lippincott's Magazine*, October, 1873.

3. Young E. Allison, "The Moonshine Men," *Southern Bivouac* 2 (February, 1887); William Goodell Frost, "The Southern Mountaineer: Our Kindred of the Boone and Lincoln Type," *American Monthly Review of Reviews* 21 (March, 1900): 303–11; Rollin Lynde Hart, "The Mountaineers: Our Own Lost Tribes," *Century* 95 (January, 1918): 395–404; "Poor White Trash," *Littell's Living Age* 153 (June 17, 1882): 688–91; Ellen Churchill Semple, "The Anglo-Saxons of the Kentucky Mountains," *Geographical Journal*, June, 1901.

4. Homer Bigart, "Kentucky Miners: A Grim Winter," *New York Times*, October 20, 1963.

5. Bryan Crawford, "This Man's Life Is No 'Fantasy Island,'" *Louisville Courier-Journal*, April 18, 1978.

6. James Branscome, *The Federal Government in Appalachia* (Field Foundation, 1977).

7. "Four Hundred Plan Program to Care for Appalachia's Children," *Louisville Courier-Journal*, June 5, 1977.

8. Thomas Murray, "The Investment Nobody Knows About," *Dun's Review and Modern Industry*, April, 1965; Kyle Vance, "River of Profit, Trickle of Taxes," *Louisville Courier-Journal*, August 29, 1965; James C. Millstone, "East Kentucky Coal Makes Profit for Owners, Not Region," and "Kentucky's Method of Taxing Coal Lands Is Woefully Inadequate," *St. Louis Post-Dispatch*, November 17–18, 1967.

9. Curt Brown, "West Virginia Establishment: The Affluent in Total Control," *Charleston Gazette*, February 7, 1971. All of this was subse-

quently described and documented in John C. Wells, Jr., "Poverty Amidst Riches: Why People Are Poor in Appalachia" (Ph.D. dissertation, Rutgers University, 1977), a work which is essential reading for any serious student of political, social, and economic realities in modern America.

10. O. D. Weaver, W. L. Calvert, and W. H. McGuire, "A New Look at the Oil and Gas Potential of the Appalachian Basin," *Oil and Gas Journal*, January 17 and July 10, 1972.

11. Howard Fineman, "Owners of State's Coal Changing as Energy Firms Move In," *Louisville Courier-Journal*, December 18, 1977.

12. Quoted in Matthew Josephson, *The Robber Barons* (New York: Harcourt, Brace, 1934).

13. John T. Flynn, *God's Gold* (New York: Harcourt, Brace, 1934), p. 401.

14. Carol Crowe-Carraco, *The Big Sandy* (Lexington: University Press of Kentucky, 1979), pp. 77–84.

15. Paul Camplin, *Strip Mining in Kentucky* (Commonwealth of Kentucky, Strip Mining and Reclamation Commission, 1965), p. 6.

16. Stewart Holbrook, *The Age of the Moguls* (Garden City, N.Y.: Doubleday, 1953).

Chapter One, "Why the Moguls Came"

1. *Description of a Tract of Timber, Coal and Agricultural Land, in Breathitt County, Kentucky, Containing 67,000 acres with Reports on the same from State Geologists of Kentucky, and others, with an Abstract of the Title appended* (Urbana, Ill.: James F. Hearne, Printer, 1885). Copy in University of Kentucky Geology Library, Lexington.

2. James Lane Allen, "Through Cumberland Gap on Horseback," *Harper's* 73 (June, 1886): 50–66; James Lane Allen, "Mountain Passes of the Cumberland," *Harper's* 81 (September, 1890): 561–76; William Perry Brown, "A Peculiar People," *Overland Monthly Magazine*, November, 1888; John C. Campbell, *The Southern Highlander and His Homeland* (New York: Russell Sage Foundation, 1921).

3. Willard Rouse Jillson, "History of the Kentucky Geological Survey, 1838–1921," *Register of the Kentucky Historical Society* 19:57; William W. Mather, "Report on the Geological Reconnaisance of Kentucky, Made in 1838," *Journal of the Kentucky Senate* (1839); David Dale Owen, *Kentucky Geological Survey, 1854–57*; Nathaniel Southgate Shaler, *Kentucky Geological Survey, 1873–80*; John Robert Proctor, *Kentucky Geological Survey, 1880–92*; Nathaniel Southgate

Shaler, *Kentucky: A Pioneer Commonwealth* (Boston: Houghton Mifflin, 1884); J. W. Huddle et al., *Coal Reserves of Eastern Kentucky* (Washington, D.C.: U.S. Government Printing Office, 1963); Mary Verhoeff, "The Kentucky Mountains: Transportation and Commerce, 1750–1911," Filson Club Paper No. 26 (Louisville, 1911); Mary Verhoeff, "The Kentucky River Navigation," Filson Club Paper No. 28 (Louisville, 1917).

4. Charles E. Beachley, *History of the Consolidation Coal Company* (n.p.: Consolidation Coal Company, 1924); Crowe-Carraco, *Big Sandy*; Henry P. Scalf, *Kentucky's Last Frontier* (Prestonburg, Ky.: Adams Press, 1966), pp. 327–37.

5. Scalf, *Kentucky's Last Frontier*; William Elsey Connelly, *The Founding of Harman's Station and the Wiley Captivity*, reprint ed. (n.p.: Harman Station Publishers, 1966).

6. Joyce Wilson, *This Was Yesterday: A Romantic History of Owsley County, Kentucky* (Ashland, Ky.: Economy Printers, 1977).

Chapter Two, "Middlesborough: The Magic City"

1. John H. Ward, "The Eleventh Tennessee Infantry," *Confederate Veteran* 16 (1908): 420.

2. *Cumberland Gap*, Picturesque America, Series D (n.p.: Appleton, 1872).

3. Allen, "Through Cumberland Gap on Horseback."

4. Robert L. Kincaid, *The Wilderness Road* (Harrogate, Tenn.: Lincoln Memorial University Press, 1955).

5. Ibid., p. 315.

6. Dave Colson was a man of much charm and magnetism. He was also a college graduate, a great rarity in the Kentucky hills at the time. He took his money and ran successfully for Congress, where he zealously served the interests of the American Association, Ltd. In January, 1900, he killed a man in a pistol duel in the crowded lobby of the Capitol Hotel in Frankfort—but that is another story. See L. F. Johnson, *Famous Kentucky Trials and Tragedies* (n.p.: Baldwin Law Book Company, 1916), pp. 292–300.

7. Charles Blanton Roberts, "The Building of Middlesboro: A Notable Epoch in the History of Eastern Kentucky," *Filson Club Historical Quarterly* 7 (1933): 21.

8. Ibid., p. 25.

9. Landon H. Smalling, *Middlesboro and Before Middlesboro Was* (Louisville: George F. Fetter, 1924), p. 20.

10. Roberts, "Building," p. 28.

11. A. J. Rosenbalm III, "Observations on Middlesborough, Kentucky" (unpublished paper, University of Kentucky, 1981).

12. Roberts, "Building," p. 29; Kincaid, *Wilderness Road*, p. 329; Charles T. Rogers, "Dreams of English Optimists Who Had Visions of an Imperial City Are Coming True," *Thousand Sticks Journal* (Middlesborough, Ky.), November 9, 1911.

13. Roberts, "Building"; Kincaid, *Wilderness Road*.

14. Rosenbalm, "Observations."

15. Kincaid, *Wilderness Road*, pp. 335, 336.

16. Ibid., pp. 333–39.

17. Ibid., p. 337.

18. *Picturesque Middlesboro—the Magic City* (Middlesboro: Pinnacle Printery, ca. 1914).

19. J. C. Tipton, *The Cumberland Coal Field and Its Creators* (Middlesboro: Pinnacle Printery, 1905), pp. 1–10; see also *Picturesque Middlesboro*.

20. Stuart Seely Sprague, "The Great Appalachian Iron and Coal Town Boom of 1889–1893," *Appalachian Journal* (Spring 1977).

21. John O'Callaghan, "War on Beauty," *Manchester Guardian*, July 10, 1965.

22. John Gaventa, "The Unknown Lowson Empire," *Social Audit* (London) 4 (Spring 1974): 18–31. See also his *Power and Powerlessness: Quiescence and Rebellion in an Appalachian Valley* (Urbana: University of Illinois Press, 1980), pp. 237–49.

Other sources important in the story of Middlesborough include Jillson, *Coal Industry in Kentucky*; the official records of Bell County and the City of Middlesboro; the archives of the *Middlesboro Daily News*; and Allen, "Mountain Passes of the Cumberland."

Chapter Three, "The First Moguls"

1. Helen Matthews Lewis, Linda Johnson, and Don Askins, eds., *Colonialism in Modern America: The Appalachian Case* (Boone, N.C.: Consortium Press, 1978).

2. B. F. Johnson, *Men of Mark in Maryland* (Baltimore: Baltimore Press, 1910), p. 331.

3. Edward Hungerford, *The Story of the Baltimore and Ohio Railroad, 1827–1927* (New York: G. P. Putnam's Sons, 1928).

4. Katherine A. Harvey, *The Best Dressed Miners: Life and Labor in the Maryland Coal Region, 1835–1910* (Ithaca, N.Y.: Cornell University Press, 1969), pp. 3–14.

5. Arthur Lewell, *Borden Mining Company: A Brief History* (Frostburg, Md.: Frostburg Printing, 1938).

6. Harvey, *Best Dressed Miners*, ch. 1.

7. "Warren Delano," *National Cyclopedia of American Biography*, XXXIV, 55. So great was the influence of the Roosevelt and Delano families in the councils of the Maryland operators that in 1899, when Theodore Roosevelt, then the strongly anti-labor governor of New York, spoke in Frostburg the miners were given a holiday and ordered to go and hear him.

8. Harvey, *Best Dressed Miners* p. 11; Beachley, *History of Consolidation Coal*, pp. 8–22.

9. "Harry Crawford Black," *National Cyclopedia of American Biography*, VI, 94.

10. "John Murray Forbes," ibid., XXXV, 331–33.

11. "James Roosevelt," ibid., XXIV, 11–12.

12. "Robert Garrett," ibid., IV, 575.

13. *New York Evening Post*, October 22, 1860; quoted in Harvey, *Best Dressed Miners*, p. 33.

Chapter Four, "The Fairmont Ring"

1. W. L. Balderson, *Fort Prickett Frontier and Marion County* (n.p.: Fairmont Bicentennial Committee, ca. 1978); Franklin Marion Brand, *The William Fleming Family* (n.p.: Matthews Printing, 1941); Phil Conley, *History of the West Virginia Coal Industry* (Charleston: Educational Foundation, 1960), pp. 152–74; Glenn D. Lough, *Now and Long Ago* (Fairmont: Marion County Historical Society, 1969); *Marion County Centennial Yearbook, 1863–1963* (Fairmont, ca. 1964); James O. Watson, "Marion County in the Making," published by the Fairmont High School Class of 1916; James Otis Watson II, "The Valley Coal Story," *Times-West Virginian*, February 3, 1956; reprinted by Fairmont Printing, ca. 1978.

2. Hungerford, *The Story of the Baltimore & Ohio*, I, 257–67.

3. Beachley, *History of Consolidation Coal*, pp. 37–42; John Alexander Williams, *West Virginia and the Captains of Industry* (Morgantown: West Virginia Foundation, 1976); William Graebner, *Coal Mining Safety in the Progressive Era* (Lexington: University Press of Kentucky, 1976), pp. 112–54.

4. "Johnson Newlon Camden, Sr.," *Dictionary of American Biography*, II, 43; also Johnson Newlon Camden, Sr., Papers, University of West Virginia Archives, Morgantown.

5. Hildegarde Dolson, *The Great Oildorado* (New York: Random House, 1959).

6. Festus Summers, *Johnson Newlon Camden: A Study in Individualism* (New York: G. P. Putnam's Sons, 1937).

7. Howard B. Lee, *The Burning Springs and Other Tales of the Little Kanawha* (Morgantown: West Virginia University Press, 1968); Williams, *West Virginia and the Captains of Industry*.

8. Beachley, *History of Consolidation Coal*.

9. Lacy Dillon, *They Died in the Darkness* (Parsons, W.Va.: McClain Printing, 1976), pp. 68–92.

10. Graebner, *Coal Mining Safety*, p. 115.

11. Williams, *West Virginia and the Captains of Industry*, p. 192.

12. Ibid., pp. 138–39, 147, 149, 183, 198, 212.

13. "Aretas Brooks Fleming," *Dictionary of American Biography*, III, 459.

14. Williams, *West Virginia and the Captains of Industry*; "Clarence Watson," *Coal Age Magazine*, June, 1940; *Marion County Centennial Yearbook*; Watson, "The Valley Coal Story."

15. Beachley, *History of Consolidation Coal*, pp. 49–53.

Chapter Five, *"The Strange Rise of John C. C. Mayo"*

1. Verhoeff, "The Kentucky Mountains."

2. Semple, "The Anglo-Saxons of the Kentucky Mountains."

3. Sam Cowan, *Sergeant York and His People* (New York: Funk and Wagnalls, 1922); Gerald Griffin, *The Greatest American Hero* (n.p.: Commercial Printing, n.d.), copy in Wilson Collection, King Library, University of Kentucky.

4. K. S. Sol Warren, *A History of Knox County, Kentucky* (n.p., 1976), pp. 109–17.

5. John E. Buckingham, "Sketch of the Life of John C. C. Mayo," memoir, Mayo Family Papers, Ashland, Ky.

6. Mary L. Chapman, "The Influence of Coal in the Big Sandy Valley" (Ph.D. dissertation, University of Kentucky, 1945).

7. Buckingham, "Sketch of Mayo."

8. *Official Reports of the Proceedings and Debates of the Convention Assembled at Frankfort on the 8th Day of September, 1890, to Adopt, Amend, or Change the Constitution of the State of Kentucky*, IV, 4702–3, 4835–44, 4848–56, 4865.

9. Buckingham, "Sketch of Mayo."

10. Temple Bodley, "John Caldwell Calhoun Mayo," in *Bodley's His-*

tory of Kentucky (Chicago: S. J. Clark, 1928); "Death Claims John C. C. Mayo," *Big Sandy News* (Louisa, Ky.), May 18, 1914.

11. Buckingham, "Sketch of Mayo"; "Leonidas Merritt," *Dictionary of American Biography*, VI, 571–72; Peter Collier and David Horowitz, *The Rockefellers: An American Dynasty* (New York: Holt, Rinehart and Winston, 1976), pp. 54–55; Flynn, *God's Gold*, pp. 312–16.

12. Buckingham, "Sketch of Mayo"; Dwight Bratcher, "Old Time Operators," *Kentucky Coal Journal*, February, 1976.

13. Lynn Galloway, "John C. C. Mayo" (unpublished paper, University of Kentucky, 1978); *Louisville Courier-Journal*, May 11, 12, 1911; *Lexington Herald*, May 15, 1914; Buckingham, "Sketch of Mayo."

14. Buckingham, "Sketch of Mayo." For an example of Mayo's mineral purchases, see deed of conveyance from Benjamin McCray and Mahalia McCray, his wife, to Northern Coal & Coke Company, dated April 3, 1903, and of record in the Letcher County Court Clerk's office at Whitesburg, Ky. This type of deed was used to purchase several hundred tracts of minerals and mining rights in the eastern Kentucky coal field.

15. Galloway, "Mayo."

Chapter Six, "The Ring Closes In"

1. Williams, *West Virginia and the Captains of Industry*.

2. Thomas D. Clark, *Kentucky: Land of Contrast* (New York: Harper & Row, 1968), pp. 197–206.

3. Summers, *Camden*.

4. Jere Wheelwright to George C. Jenkins, October 25, 1909, in Johnson Newlon Camden, Sr., Personal Papers, University of West Virginia Library, Morgantown. Other pertinent papers held in the same library include those of Aretas Brooks Fleming, governor of the state from 1890 to 1894.

5. Chapman, *Influence of Coal*, p. 205.

6. Buckingham, "Sketch of Mayo."

7. Ibid., pp. 11–12; Chapman, *Influence of Coal*, pp. 208–9.

8. Beachley, *History of Consolidation Coal*, pp. 57–62; Bratcher, "Old Time Operators"; Henry C. Scalf, "History of a Legal Strait Jacket," *Mountain Eagle*, October 14, 1973.

9. Maury Klein, *History of the Louisville & Nashville Railroad* (New York: Macmillan, 1972), pp. 312–13, 401–5; "The Kentenia Corporation," *Harlan* (Ky.) *Enterprise*, April 10, 1908, special supplement, p. 11.

10. Brian McGinty, "Oscar of the Waldorf," in *The Palace Inns* (Harrisburg, Pa.: Stackpole Books, 1978), pp. 170–80.

11. Buckingham, "Sketch of Mayo"; author's interview with Harry LaViers, Sr.

12. James Terrill Wilson's interview with Ivan Kimbrell, 1978, Neon, Ky.

13. Chapman, *Influence of Coal*, pp. 208–10.

14. Elizabeth Wassum Dramcyzk, "History of Jenkins, Kentucky," published by Jenkins Area Jaycees, 1973; Alphonse Broskey, "Building a Town for a Mountain Community: A Glimpse of Jenkins and Nearby Villages," *Coal Age*, April 5, 1923; "Jenkins Is Model Mining Town," *Lexington Herald*, January 9, 1921; Thomas B. A. Keleman, "A History of Lynch, Kentucky (Master's thesis, University of Kentucky, 1972); Malcolm Ross, *Machine Age in the Hills* (New York: Macmillan, 1933); Beachley, *History of Consolidation Coal*.

15. "George Carrell Jenkins," *National Cyclopedia of American Biography*, XXVII, 317–18.

16. Joe Creason, "A Captive City Is Set Free," *Louisville Courier-Journal*, April 3, 1949.

17. "Samuel McRoberts," *National Cyclopedia of American Biography*, XXXVI, 194–95.

18. Harvey, *Best Dressed Miners*, p. 11; Arthur M. Schlesinger, *The Crisis of the Old Order* (Cambridge: Harvard University Press, 1957), II, 356.

19. "Inspection Trip of the Directors and Their Friends of the Elk Horn," illustrated promotional brochure of Elk Horn Mining Company, 1914; copy in Special Collections, Margaret I. King Library, University of Kentucky. See also Desha Breckinridge, "Stores of Wealth Untold Lie in Rich Coal Fields of Eastern Kentucky," *Lexington Herald*, December 10, 11, 1910.

20. Buckingham, "Sketch of Mayo"; "Clarence Wayland Watson," *National Cyclopedia of American Biography*, XXXI, 359–60.

21. Howard B. Lee, *Bloodletting in Appalachia* (Parsons, W.Va.: McClain Printing, 1969), p. 143.

22. "Watson Out as Coal Company Head," *New York Times*, February 7, 1911, p. 2.

23. Buckingham, "Sketch of Mayo," pp.16–17; "Eastern Kentucky Coal Lands Corporation *v.* Commonwealth of Kentucky," 106 *Southwestern Reporter* 260 (December 20, 1907); "John C. C. Mayo Yields to Ills," *Louisville Courier-Journal*, May 12, 1914.

24. Galloway, "Mayo"; Scalf, "History of a Legal Strait Jacket"; "John C. C. Mayo," *National Cyclopedia of American Biography*,

XXVI, 194–95; Bodley, "Mayo," in *Bodley's History of Kentucky*, pp. 356–60.

25. "Mayo Yields to Ills."

26. Charles Dahlenburg, "John C. C. Mayo's Mansion," *Paintsville Herald*, April 26, 1978.

27. Buckingham, "Sketch of Mayo," p. 14; "C. Bascom Slemp," *Dictionary of American Biography*, suppl. 3, pp. 714–15.

28. *Louisville Courier-Journal*, May 12, 1914. Judge Allie Young of Morehead, Kentucky, was one of Mayo's closest friends and confidants. Commenting on the tragedy of Mayo's death, he noted that when he became ill the tycoon was working on a deal that would have eclipsed anything he had previously accomplished: "It was a gigantic one. . . . Had he lived to put through the deal it would have been only a few years until he would have been in a class with John Pierpont Morgan."

29. Ibid.

30. James Terrell Wilson, interview with John C. C. Mayo, Jr., 1978, Ashland, Ky.

31. George S. McGovern and Leonard Guttredge, *The Great Coalfield War* (Boston: Houghton Mifflin, 1972), pp. 76–77.

32. "John Mayo Dies In New York," *Lexington Herald*, May 12, 1914.

33. *Bodley's History of Kentucky*, pp. 358–60.

Chapter Seven, "The Kingdom of Lynch"

1. Allen, "Mountain Passes of the Cumberland."

2. "Kentenia Corporation," *Harlan Enterprise*, April 10, 1908.

3. Mabel Green Condon, *A History of Harlan County* (Knoxville: Parthenon Press, 1962), pp. 10–14.

4. Eleanor Roosevelt, *This Is My Story* (New York: Harper & Brothers, 1937).

5. James Otis Watson II, *The Valley Coal Story* (Fairmont: Fairmont Printing, 1957), pp. 3–4.

6. Mabel Brown Ellis, "Children of the Kentucky Coal Fields," *American Child* 11 (1920): 321–22; Ross, *Machine Age in the Hills*.

7. "Fordson Mine," *Coal Age* 36 (March, 1931): 129–30.

8. Paul Frederick Cressy, "Social Disorganization and Reorganization in Harlan County, Kentucky," *American Sociological Review* 14 (June, 1949): 389–94.

9. Campbell, *Southern Highlander and His Homeland*.

10. Collier and Horowitz, *Rockefellers*, pp. 53–55; Flynn, *God's Gold*, pp. 313–14; Josephson, *Robber Barons*, p. 397.

11. Ferdinand Lundberg, *America's Sixty Families* (New York: Vanguard, 1937), pp. 196–97.

12. Albert Pearce, "The Growth and Overdevelopment of the Kentucky Coal Industry" (Master's thesis, University of Kentucky, 1930).

13. Deed of conveyance, Deed Book no. 33, p. 395, Harlan County, Ky., Public Records.

14. Howard N. Eavenson, "Lynch Plant of United States Coal and Coke Company," *Transactions* of the American Institute of Mining and Metallurgical Engineers 57 (1922); 653ff.; Ellis, "Children of Kentucky Coal Fields," pp. 333, 374; Rose C. Field, "What I Found in Lynch, Kentucky," *Success Magazine*, March, 1926.

15. Keleman, "History of Lynch"; also *Middlesboro Pinnacle*, October 29, 1917, October 26, 1918; *Middlesboro Daily News*, March 5, 1924, October 20, 1926; *Harlan Enterprise*, November 27, 1925, July 23, 1926; *Big Stone Gap* (Va.) *Post*, October 10, 1917, April 8, 1926; *Tri-City News* (Cumberland, Ky.), March 28, April 4, June 20, 1930.

16. Alphonse Brosky, "Lynch Coal Buried in Places 3500 Feet Deep" and "Lynch Mine, Its Record Production and Operating Data," *Coal Age*, October 11, 1923.

17. Alphonse Brosky, "A Glimpse of Jenkins, Kentucky, and Nearby Villages," *Coal Age*, April 5, 1923; Creason, "Captive City Is Set Free."

18. Leonard W. Levy, ed., *Harlan Miners Speak: Report on Terrorism in the Kentucky Coal Fields* (New York: Harcourt, Brace, 1932); George Titler, *Hell in Harlan* (Beckley, W.Va.: BJW Printers, 1974).

19. Holbrook, *Age of the Moguls*.

20. Keleman, "History of Lynch"; "Thomas Lynch," *National Cyclopedia of American Biography*, XVI, 88–89.

Chapter Eight, "The Rich and Mighty Capitalists"

1. Daniel Allen, "Mine War in Pennsylvania," *The Nation*, August 16, 1933; Joe Daniel Carr, "Labor Conflict in the Eastern Kentucky Coal Fields," *Filson Club Historical Quarterly*, April, 1973; Stirling D. Spero and Jacob Aranoff, "War in the Kentucky Mountains," *American Mercury*, February, 1932; Maurer Maurer and Calvin F. Senning, *Billy Mitchell, the Air Service and the Mingo War* (Montgomery, Ala.: Air Force Historical Foundation, 1965).

2. Wayne Broehl, *The Molly Maguires* (Cambridge: Harvard University Press, 1964), p. 340.

3. Holbrook, *Age of the Moguls*.

4. David Alan Corbin, *Life, Work, and Rebellion in the Coal Fields* (Urbana: University of Illinois Press, 1981); Winthrop Lane, *Civil War in West Virginia: The Story of Industrial Conflict in the Coal Mines* (n.p.: B. W. Hubsch, 1922); Lee, *Bloodletting*; Fred Mooney, *Struggle in the Coal Fields* (Morgantown: West Virginia University Press, 1967).

5. Jennie Lee, "A Diary from a Kentucky Mining Camp," *World Tomorrow* 15 (March, 1932); "In the Driftway," *The Nation*, June 8, 1932; "News from the Front," *Survey*, October 15, 1931; Charles R. Walker, "'Red' Blood in Kentucky," *Forum* 87 (January, 1932); Titler, *Hell in Harlan*; John W. Hevener, *Which Side Are You On?* (Urbana: University of Illinois Press, 1978); *Harlan and Bell Counties, Kentucky, 1921–32* (Huntington, W.Va.: Appalachian Movement Press, 1972).

6. Jim Garland, "The Death of Harry Simms," on, e.g., Pete Seeger, *Essential Pete Seeger*, Vanguard (S)VSD-97/98, 1978; Aunt Molly Jackson, "Poor Miner's Farewell," on *The Songs and Stories of Aunt Molly Jackson*, stories told by Aunt Molly Jackson, songs sung by John Greenway, Folkways FH 5457, 1961; Sarah Gunning, "I Hate the Capitalist System," on *The Silver Dagger*, Rounder 0051, n.d.; Aunt Molly Jackson, "Join the CIO," on *Aunt Molly Jackson*, Rounder 1002, n.d. (This song was originally entitled "Join the NMU," and was a plea for membership in the communist National Miners Union. After the New Deal it was revised and became an important rallying song in the CIO's organizational campaigns.)

7. Ronald D. Eller, "The Coal Barons of the Appalachian South," *Appalachian Journal* 4 (Spring-Summer 1977); Ellis, "Children of the Coal Fields."

8. Bob Hill, "Garden Spot: Coal Miner Recalls Old Days When Coal Boomed," *Louisville Courier-Journal*, November 8, 1978; Alphonse Brosky, "Sociological Work Accomplished by the Consolidation Coal Company," *Coal Age*, January 9, 1919.

9. Wells, "Poverty Amidst Riches."

10. Ross, *Machine Age in the Hills*; Homer Lawrence Morris, *The Plight of the Bituminous Coal Miner* (Philadelphia: University of Pennsylvania Press, 1934); Levy, *Harlan Miners Speak*; Walter H. Hamilton and Helen R. Wright, *The Case of Bituminous Coal* (New York: Macmillan, 1925); Homer Greene, *Coal and the Coal Mines* (Boston: Houghton Mifflin, 1928); Pearce, "Growth and Overdevelopment of the Kentucky Coal Industry"; "Survey of the Coal Industry," *Survey Graphic* 27 (March 25, 1922).

11. Harvey O'Connor, *Mellon's Millions: The Life and Times of Andrew W. Mellon* (New York: John Day, 1933), pp. 402–21.

12. "Charles E. Hellier," *National Cyclopedia of American Biography*, XV, 348.

13. "Augustus Foscoe Whitfield," ibid., XXXVI, 510–11.

14. "Howard N. Eavenson," ibid., XXXIX, 554–55.

15. "Robert Lyon Stearns," ibid., XXXI, 472.

16. "George C. Westervelt," ibid., XXXIII, 103–4.

17. Harvey O'Connor's *Mellon's Millions* remains the best study of this ruthless family and its fanatical, methodical, almost insane drive for money in sums so large as to surpass comprehension. See also Burton Hersh, *The Mellon Family: A Fortune in History* (New York: William Morrow, 1978).

18. "J. Gardner Bradley," *National Cyclopedia of American Biography*, LVI, 164–65.

19. See the following: "The folk culture of the Kentucky Cumberlands," *The Dial*, January 31, 1918; "Hobnobbing with Hillbillies," *Harper's*, December, 1915; "In Shakespeare's America," ibid., August, 1915; "The Women on Troublesome," *Scribner's*, March, 1918; *Singing Carr* (New York: Alfred A. Knopf, 1918).

20. William Aspinwall Bradley, *Old Christmas and Other Kentucky Tales* (Boston: Houghton Mifflin, 1917).

Chapter Nine, "After the Ball Was Over"

1. Interview with Riley Mullins, June, 1971.

2. Josephson, *Robber Barons*.

3. "Hazard Attorney Describes How Barons Seek to Control Politics," *Louisville Courier-Journal*, July 31, 1923.

4. Collier and Horowitz, *Rockefellers*, p. 69.

5. Anna Rochester, *Labor and Coal* (New York: International, 1931), p. 63.

6. Lee, *Bloodletting*; McGovern and Guttredge, *Great Coal Field War*; Mooney, *Struggle in the Coal Fields*; Winthrop D. Lane, "The Black Avalanche," *Survey* 47 (March 25, 1922); "The Insurrection in Tennessee," *Harper's* 36 (August 27, 1892); Charles Frederick Carter, "Murder to Maintain Coal Monopoly," *Current History* 15 (January 1922).

7. Rochester, *Labor and Coal*, p. 243; Ross, *Machine Age in the Hills*, p. 53.

8. John Day, *Bloody Ground* (New York: Doubleday, Doran, 1941); Lewis W. Field, Reed T. Ewing, and David M. Wayne, "Observations

on the Relation of Psychological Factors to Psychiatric Disorders among Coal Miners," *International Journal of Social Psychiatry* 3 (1957): 133–45; Carl Wiesel and Malcolm Arny, "A Psychiatric Study of Coal Miners in the Eastern Kentucky Area," *American Journal of Psychiatry* 108 (February, 1952): 617–24; Richard Louv, "The Appalachian Syndrome," *Human Behavior*, May, 1977; Paul Frederick Cressey, "Social Disorganization and Reorganization in Harlan County, Kentucky," *American Sociological Review* 14 (June, 1949).

9. Ross, *Machine Age in the Hills*, p. 58.

10. Watson, *Valley Coal Story*.

11. Ivan Kimbrell has said that on one occasion (when he was somewhat tipsy) Watson declared that his elevation to the Senate in 1911 cost him a million dollars; on another occasion the senator lamented the loss of $16,000,000 in the Crash.

12. Lee, *Bloodletting*, pp. 143–46.

13. Beachley, *History of Consolidation Coal*, pp. 67–78.

14. "Clarence W. Watson Passes," *Coal Age* 45 (June, 1940).

15. Laura Ridenour, "High Gate Is Show Case of Marion County History," *Times-West Virginian* (Fairmont, W.Va.), January 13, 1980; Laura Ridenour, "Fairmont Farms Once Spanish Mission Style Showplace," ibid., March 9, 1980.

16. Dahlenburg, "Mayo's Mansion."

17. Melvin Dubofsky and Warren Van Tine, *John L. Lewis* (New York: Quadrangle/New York Times, 1977; Urbana: University of Illinois Press, 1983); Joseph E. Finley, *The Corrupt Kingdom* (New York: Simon & Schuster, 1972); Trevor Armbrister, *Act of Vengeance* (New York: Saturday Review Press/E. P. Dutton, 1975); Brit Hume, *Death in the Mines* (New York: Grossman, 1971).

18. Titler, *Hell in Harlan*.

19. See also Dubofsky and Van Tine, *Lewis*, pp. 398–404.

20. Summers, *Camden*, pp. 568–70.

21. "Johnson Newlon Camden, Jr.," *National Cyclopedia of American Biography*, XXXII, 375.

22. Bigart, "Kentucky Miners: A Grim Winter."

23. Frank Harvey, *Nightmare County* (New York: Bantam, 1964), is a searing book about Hellier and the rest of Pike County.

Chapter Ten, "The Modern Moguls"

1. Lewis Corey, *House of Morgan* (1930; reprint, AMS Press).

2. Statement by Ray Adkins, in Democratic primary campaign against Congressman Carl Perkins.

3. Kai Erikson, *Everything in Its Path: Destruction of a Community in the Buffalo Creek Disaster* (New York: Simon & Schuster, 1978); Gerald M. Stern, *The Buffalo Creek Disaster* (New York: Random House, 1976); *Disaster on Buffalo Creek: A Citizens' Report on Criminal Negligence in a West Virginia Mining Community* (n.p., n.d.), p. 27.

4. Tom Bethell, *The Hurricane Creek Massacre* (New York: Harper & Row, 1972).

5. Ferdinand Lundberg, *The Rich and the Super-Rich* (New York: Lyle Stuart, 1968).

6. Because the immense and vital business of supplying Kentucky's mineral resources to global markets involves constant changes in corporate forms and in personal ownership and involvements, some of the situations and relationships described in this chapter may have undergone substantial change between the time of writing (1982) and publication. The ensuing analysis is based on the best available information from industries that are notoriously closed-mouthed about their affairs.

7. "No More Whales: The Gottwalds Acquired a 'Dying' Business and Built Ethyl into a Giant," *Forbes*, May 29, 1978, p. 85.

8. David Fields, "Kentucky River Coal Corporation" (unpublished paper, Department of History, University of Kentucky, 1979); Buckingham, "Sketch of Mayo."

9. Johnson Newlon Camden, Jr., Last Will and Testament, copy in Bourbon County court clerk's office, Paris, Ky.

10. "Catesby W. Clay," *Standard & Poor's Register of Corporations, Directors and Executives*.

11. Thomas Murray, "The Investment Nobody Knows About," *Dun's Review and Modern Industry*, April 1965; Wells, "Poverty Amidst Riches," p. 182.

12. "Edward B. Leisenring," *Standard & Poor's Register of Corporations and Executives*.

13. When Hazard attorney Joseph Eversole warned landowners that the mineral deeds were tantamount to fee simple conveyances, the purchasers sought to silence him; when he refused to alter his opinion, he was ambushed. In the resulting "war" Fulton French, a lawyer for the land syndicate, and at least seventeen other men were slain. The county was convulsed, the courts suspended all trials for a time, and Perry and Breathitt Counties became infamous for brutality and violence. See Eunice Tolbert Johnson, *History of Perry County, Kentucky* (Hazard: Daughters of the American Revolution, 1953), p. 57.

14. Roosevelt, *This Is My Story*. See also the public archives of Letcher, Perry, Breathitt, Knott, Leslie, and Pike Counties, where the Trigg and Horsley deeds of purchase and conveyance are recorded.

15. Wells, "Poverty Amidst Riches"; Howard Fineman, "Owners of State's Coal Changing as Energy Firms Move In," *Louisville Courier-Journal*, December 8, 1977; "Virginia Iron, Coal & Coke Company," *Moody's Industrial Manual* (1966), p. 1836.

16. Kurt McCord, "Virginia Iron, Coal & Coke Company: A Subsidiary of American Natural Resources Systems, Inc." (unpublished paper, Department of History, University of Kentucky, 1979).

17. Wells, "Poverty Amidst Riches," p. 183; Fineman, "Owners Changing."

18. "Kentucky Coal Part of Shell Unit's Venture," *Louisville Courier-Journal*, March 19, 1980.

19. Lundberg, *America's Sixty Families*.

20. "Pittston Company," *Standard & Poor's Corporate Stock Reports*, XLVI, no. 131, sec. 21, p. 1856 (July 9, 1979); Wells, "Poverty Amidst Riches," pp. 182, 189; Wayne Flint, *Dixie's Forgotten People* (Bloomington: Indiana University Press, 1979), p. 152.

21. "Calvin Nathaniel Payne," *National Cyclopedia of American Biography*, XXIV, 282–83.

22. Fineman, "Owners Changing"; Joseph Wilkinson, "Peabody Becomes Profitable Again," *Coal Age*, October, 1908; Wells, "Poverty Amidst Riches," p. 182.

23. "The Best Laid Plans," *Forbes*, June 1, 1976.

24. Fineman, "Owners Changing."

25. Brown Brothers, Harriman & Company, "Statement of Condition," June 30, 1981; Federal Election Commission, "Selected List of Receipts and Expenditures (G), Section I: Individuals," February 28, 1981, p. 3246.

26. Fineman, "Owners Changing"; Wells, "Poverty Amidst Riches"; "Land Ownership Patterns and Their Impacts on Appalachian Communities: A Survey of 80 Counties," submitted to the Appalachian Regional Commission by the Appalachian Land Ownership Task Force, Washington, D.C., February, 1981.

27. Phillip Moeller, "Ashland Oil Plans 'Major Stake' in Kentucky Coal Business," *Louisville Courier-Journal*, May 27, 1977; James Cook, "Do Coal and Oil Mix?" *Forbes*, October 15, 1977; "The Oil Majors Bet on Coal," *Business Week*, September 24, 1979; Howard Fineman, "Energy Companies Are Diversifying by Becoming Coal Producers in State," *Louisville Courier-Journal*, December 19, 1977.

28. Ed Zuckerman, "Hopkins Contributors Widely Varied," *Lexington Leader*, May 16, 1979.

29. *Corporate Data Exchange Directory No. 4: Energy* (1980).

30. Howard Fineman, "Kentucky Has Natural Gas, But There's a Catch," *Louisville Courier-Journal*, February 13, 1977; Wells, "Poverty Amidst Riches," pp. 148–52.

31. Lewis, Johnson, and Askins, eds., *Colonialism in America*.

32. *World Almanac* (1977).

33. Kaylene Haynes and David Begley, "Biography of William B. Sturgill" (unpublished paper, Department of History, University of Kentucky, 1979); John Ed Pearce, "William Sturgill, Blue Grass Biggy," *Louisville Courier-Journal*, July 1, 1979.

34. "Brown Commits to Coal: Coal Man Named Energy Chief," *Kentucky Coal Journal*, December, 1979.

35. Rena Gazaway, *The Longest Mile* (Garden City, N.Y.: Doubleday, 1969).

36. "Land Ownership Patterns," p. 46.

37. Robert T. Garrett, "Union of Two Influential Law Firms a Blissful or Barren Marriage," *Louisville Courier-Journal*, July 6, 1980.

38. "Combs Calls Appalachia a 'Major Battleground,'" ibid., April 29, 1967.

39. Fineman, "Owners Changing."

40. Richard Wilson, "Brown Expands Educational Panel, Leaving Out College Presidents," ibid., July 9, 1980.

41. Livingston Taylor, "Brown Says Free Plane Is Sort of 'Flexibility' He Needs in His Job," ibid., September 30, 1980.

42. Bob Johnson, "Coal Industry Is Holding an Appreciation Fund-Raiser for Ford," ibid., September 19, 1980.

43. "Wendell Ford: The Senator from Coal Is Running a Grueling Campaign," *Lexington Herald-Leader*, October 12, 1980; see also Johnson, "Fund-Raiser for Ford."

44. *Corporate Data Exchange Directory No. 4: Energy*. For a worthwhile analysis of this work, see Vic Reinemer, "The Dominant Dozen: Who Owns Energy Corporations?" *Public Power*, November-December, 1980.

45. Two other works of much general interest on the modern moguls of central Appalachia are Tom D. Miller, *Who Owns West Virginia?* (Huntington: Huntington Publishing, 1974), and Lee Mueller, "State Government Often Coal Industry's Silent Partner," *Lexington Sunday Herald-Leader*, February 14, 1982. The estimates of Fineman, Wells, and other writers of the acreages owned by Appalachian energy

companies are based on tax records and similar sources that are almost invariably low. For example, it is frequently reported that U.S. Steel owns 29,000 acres in eastern Kentucky, but a spokesman for the corporation told a group of visiting students and professors from the University of Kentucky in 1979 that the holdings included 41,000 acres.

Index

A Note on the Author

HARRY M. CAUDILL came to national prominence in 1963 with the publication of *Night Comes to the Cumberlands*. He followed that book with a continuing series of articles in such magazines as the *Atlantic Monthly, The Nation, New York Times Sunday Magazine, Audubon Magazine, Commonweal, Mountain Life and Work,* and many others. He has testified before both houses of Congress on such public issues as balanced economic development, strip mining, and the problems of older Americans in rural areas. His other books include *My Land Is Dying* (1971), *A Darkness at Dawn: Appalachian Kentucky and the Future* (1976), and *The Watches of the Night* (1976). He has also written two novels: *Dark Hills to Westward: The Saga of Jennie Wiley* and *The Senator from Slaughter County*. His most recent book is *The Mountain, the Miner, and the Lord* (1980).